Praise for *Preaching Happiness*

"Ginny Sassaman's down-to-earth wisdom both elevates and elates . . . an important voice in our quest for a more just and joyful world."

> — TAL BEN-SHAHAR, bestselling author, co-founder
> and chief learning officer of Happiness Studies
> Academy, Potentialife, Maytiv, and Happier.TV

"When I hear the word 'sermon,' I think of serious, solemn words. But Ginny Sassaman's sermons are nothing of the sort: they are entertaining, and easily draw you into the subject, which she has studied in depth. They tell us something we probably do not know about the one experience we all long for, the Holy Grail of Holy Grails: happiness. When you read this book expect the unexpected, and be ready for ideas that will change you and lead you closer to the fulfilment you are thirsty for."

> — PIERO FERRUCCI, author of *Beauty and the Soul:*
> *The Extraordinary Power of Everyday Beauty to Heal*
> *Your Life* and *The Power of Kindness: The Unexpected*
> *Benefits Of Leading A Compassionate Life*

"Ginny Sassaman knows happiness! As a co-founder of Gross National Happiness USA and a participant in the national Happiness Walk, she's been studying the subject for many years. Her approach in these marvelous sermons is both personal and social—she knows we need to change both our behaviors and some of the policies that are wreaking havoc on our planet while actually making us less happy. She doesn't shy away from the tougher questions. I especially like her sermon on beauty, an issue of quality of life that has been too often ignored in happiness research, surveys and action. But I found great value in all of them and I think you, dear reader, will too. Don't miss this book!"

— JOHN DE GRAAF, filmmaker, co-founder of
The Happiness Alliance and co-author of the
bestselling *Affluenza: The All-Consuming Epidemic*

"In clear and no uncertain terms Ginny Sassaman lays out for us the significant and uplifting reasons we all ought to be investing in happiness while building the internal life of goodness we all seek to find inside the temples of our living. With each sermon she reminds us that neither happiness, nor goodness, nor meaning are spectator sports. They require the commitment of our entire being, soul, body, mind, heart and all. Her words are all the more powerful as she herself models the opening of her very living to the cultivation of these desired states and never on behalf of herself solely; always on behalf of the larger worlds to which we each belong. We are guided here toward reflection that is life-giving, and action that is healing; there is no higher calling for a minister in my book."

— MARIA SIROIS, author of *A Short Course in*
Happiness After Loss: (and Other Dark, Difficult Times)

"Move over Gretchen Rubin. Ginny Sassaman brings at once her unique perspective, some valuable lessons, and inspiration. Each sermon is a bite size entry into positive psychology, the happiness movement, and the lovely wonderful world of Ginny Sassaman. Whether you count yourself as religious, spiritual but not religious, or atheist, this book is a fun and worthy read."

– LAURA MUSIKANSKI, executive director of the Happiness Alliance and co-author of *The Happiness Policy Handbook: How to Make Happiness and Well-Being the Purpose of Your Government*

"Ginny Sassaman's book, *Preaching Happiness: Creating a Just and Joyful World* is a gift to us who are her readers. She enables us to envision a world based on the principles of Gross National Happiness instead of a world that measures its well-being based on Gross Domestic Product. Her book is based on her own personal story of how her life has led her to uncovering the truths that she now embraces as a preacher of happiness. Her story is also one of an intellectual who looks deeply into the misguided philosophy underlying a worldview that sees ever greater economic growth as the measurement of all that is good and desirable in this world."

– ALAN R. PARKER, Native American attorney and author of *Pathways to Indigenous Nation Sovereignty: A Chronicle of Federal Policy Developments*

"If you love animals, including the human kind, then it will do your heart good to read Ginny's collected sermons. They poignantly remind us that we are all just trying to make our way in the world, that we are all connected and that our actions influence other people, animals, and the planet.

Ginny's words inspire us, give us food for thought, and provide hope that we may actually be able to find a better, more hopeful, and happier way forward. Together."

– BETH ALLGOOD, US Country Director for the
International Fund for Animal Welfare
and GNHUSA advisory board member

"Wow—a refreshing, uplifting, thought-provoking collection of stories to guide and inspire each and every one of us. Don't be shy now. Buy and enjoy. Be inspired. Happiness is coming. Moving our lives, communities, nations and planet absolutely beyond GDP."

– PAUL ROGERS, co-founder and
director of Planet Happiness

"*Preaching Happiness* is a book you will find yourself returning to again and again for its wisdom and guidance. Ginny Sassaman speaks to us with humor and passion, of life's most pressing question in this historic moment: how do we thrive together? The sermons presented here artfully combine personal story and social science research to pose new ways of thinking and living. *Preaching Happiness* will inspire you to engage in everyday practices that promote your own personal growth and fulfillment and to see new possibilities for the world we can create together."

– REV. JOAN JAVIER-DUVAL, minister of the
Unitarian Church of Montpelier, Vermont

"Ginny Sassaman combines her positive psychology knowledge, life experience, and enthusiasm for a happier world in a set of beautifully written sermons that invite the reader to reflect on their attitudes, behaviors, and decisions toward life, self and others. A must read for anyone who believes a better world is possible and is willing to take action."

— FEDERICO PAYRO, author of
Positive Project Management

"Ginny's sermons are thought-provoking and will reshape the way you perceive happiness. Not only does she skillfully spotlight the attributes that generate happiness within yourself, but she also creates a bridge between personal well-being and broader concepts such as economics and the environment. Her wisdom and personal anecdotes are exquisitely woven together and make it a joy to read."

— ARATHI RAMAPPA, global speaker,
executive & spiritual coach

"Ginny Sassaman is a true force of nature! Behind her infectious smile and quiet disposition is someone with a wealth of knowledge and wisdom who has an important message for the world to hear. Ginny delivers this message so powerfully, effortlessly and lovingly that one cannot help but listen. Her work touches the heart and inspires action. That's exactly what the world needs!"

— RANIA BADRELDIN,
founder & CEO of The Family Hub

"Ginny Sassaman is an amazing human being and her commitment to happiness, social, and environmental justice is an inspiration for us all. From the moment she begins to speak, she invites you into her hopeful and uplifting perspective of how we as individuals can begin to shift our ideas to find true happiness, collectively build a more sustainable and just world and strengthen our global connection to all living things. In these challenging times we are living in, Ginny's wisdom is a gift that will keep giving."

– RICHARD COLOMBO, producer and
community activist

"The perfect inspiration for these dystopic times."

– LAURIE FOREST, author of
The Black Witch Chronicles

"Ginny Sassaman is a happiness warrior who knows the journey AND walks the journey. Her series of secular sermons offers many paths and insights to develop our own happiness as well as to create a happiness framework for a more just and peaceful world. Actually, the world's societal and economic paradigms are shifting. People are asking for new ways of living together. *Preaching Happiness* is a timely, inspiring, and well-documented call for action."

– VALERIE FREILICH,
World Happiness Fest curator

"Ginny is a very engaging storyteller who relates to people in a very down-to-earth way. She helps listeners and readers understand the scope of happiness as an economic, political, and spiritual strategy. Generally, people react to the word 'happiness' as things that are fun, but Ginny is sharing a new understanding of the concept, one that can create a healthier planet and well-being in individuals and society."

— SHARON PARKER, strategist and
GNHUSA advisory board member

"Ginny has an excellent way of combining the interior and exterior aspects of reality, as well as the practical and spiritual nature of who and what we are as individuals, what we value, and how we should live to create a better reality for ourselves, other people, and our planet. GDP is a woefully inadequate measurement of our country's well-being. A new system, which considers more than the amount of money changing hands, should be used. Gross National Happiness is a paradigm shift worth understanding and implementing to create a *Just, Joyful World.*"

— ROBERT BEEZAT, author of *Knowing and Loving:*
The Keys to Real Happiness

"Since I've known Ginny personally and professionally for over 50 years, I can affirm that she is a 'reliable narrator'— someone you can count on to always walk her talk. And such eloquent and urgently needed talk! In these essay-sermons, she points individuals toward more fulfilling lives, and communities toward progress. As a business researcher, I am particularly excited by the potential for well-being measures to bring concord and productivity to the workplace."

— JEANNETTE CABANIS-BREWIN, co-editor,
The AMA Handbook of
Project Management, Fifth Edition

"Ginny Sassaman shares several practical lessons on the importance of bringing happiness more fully into our collective consciousness. Through very accessible storytelling, Sassaman speaks to the urgency with which we must create the conditions that support the well-being of people, animals, and the planet. This book serves both as an excellent primer for all who seek to increase their own levels of happiness, as well as a refreshing validation for those who have been steeped in the Gross National Happiness movement for years. It is a collection of sermons every book club should have on their list."

— PAULA FRANCIS, GNHUSA co-founder

"Ginny Sassaman is the poster lady for happiness in action. But she's not about creating escapist fantasies of happiness. She's a clear-eyed, doing-oriented 'love warrior,' who believes in facing the scariest parts of life with a deep breath, patience, compassion, more deep breaths, and the willingness to step up and get her hands dirty and her heart sore in order to make the world a better place to hang out in during our short, sweet lives."

— KATHRYN BLUME, co-founder of
the community climate game *Vermontivate*

"This book is first and foremost practical. These are the kinds of sermons with the potential to inform your choices during the work week. Ginny has a way of making it real that you can take into your real world. Read this and be inspired to make better choices for yourself and those you love."

– DR. KARISSA THACKER, founder and president of Strategic Performance Solutions, and author of *The Art of Authenticity: Tools to Become an Authentic Leader and Your Best Self*

"Ginny Sassaman is a visionary of good will. Her sermons inspire introspection and hope in a time when we must find ways to hold a strong, kind, loving and patient stance in this rapidly changing world."

– KAYLA BECKER, BCTMB, ATMAT

"*Preaching Happiness* covers all the aspects of a happy life. . . . Read it and more importantly, live it!"

– BRACO POBRIC, author of *Habits and Happiness: How to Become Happier and Improve Your Wellbeing by Changing Your Habits*

Preaching Happiness

Creating a Just and Joyful World

Judy,
Wishing you + the planet much happiness! + well being!
Ginny S—

Ginny Sassaman

Dearest Judy — I am so grateful to know you, and am blessed you are my friend. Much happiness to you.
Barbara
June 2020

Rootstock Publishing

First Printing: May 29, 2020

PREACHING HAPPINESS: CREATING A JUST AND JOYFUL WORLD
Copyright © 2020 by Ginny Sassaman
All Rights Reserved.

ISBN: 978-1-57869-026-8
eISBN: 978-1-57869-029-9
LCCN: 2019920792

Published by Rootstock Publishing
an imprint of Multicultural Media, Inc.
27 Main Street, Suite 6
Montpelier, VT 05602
www.rootstockpublishing.com
info@rootstockpublishing.com

Email the author at preachinghappiness@gmail.com.

Cover artwork by Mary Hill, maryhillstudios.com.
Cover and interior design by D. Hoffman.

Printed in the USA

While I have been blessed with many loved ones and teachers, there is really only one person to whom I can dedicate this book: the man whose unconditional love and support for me since we were both teenagers have made my life's explorations possible, my husband, Robert Edward Sassaman.

Table of Contents

Acknowledgments

The knowledge, wisdom, skill, commitment, and love of so many people are contained within this book.

First, I want to acknowledge the growth and pioneering spirit I've been fortunate to share with my Gross National Happiness USA friends and colleagues, especially the founders group: Tom Barefoot, Paula Francis, and Linda Wheatley, along with our Happiness Alliance founders and friends, Laura Musikanski and John de Graaf. I must also tip my hat to the late Eric Zencey, a central Vermont scholar, GNHUSA ally, and writer whose "G.D.P. R.I.P." op-ed in the *New York Times* was crucially important to my understanding of our mission.

Our work would not have been possible without the historic efforts of the citizens of Bhutan, the first country to espouse and adopt a Gross National Happiness system. Their bold decision is a gift to the entire world.

Thanks, too, to Eric Weiner, whose book *The Geography of Bliss* first introduced me to the GNH concept. It was a lightning bolt moment, eventually transforming my life.

I am grateful to Dr. Lynn Johnson, who led a one-day seminar on personal happiness in Burlington, Vermont, in 2010. Our paths have never again crossed but his teaching was obviously inspiring, since I haven't stopped studying the subject since.

Without a doubt, my most important happiness teacher has been Tal Ben-Shahar. I had heard of Ben-Shahar's wildly popular positive psychology course at Harvard, and wished I could somehow take it. When I learned that he and his colleagues Maria Sirois and Meghan McDonough, of the Wholebeing Institute, were offering a yearlong Certificate in Positive Psychology program, I signed up immediately. To pay for the course, I had to take money out of my retirement fund, a decision I will never regret. I live the CiPP teachings every day. My gratitude for Tal, Maria, and Meghan runs deep.

My graduate studies in mediation and conflict resolution also shaped who I am and how I behave on a daily basis. In particular, Susanne Terry and Alice Estey not only taught me the fundamentals of conflict theory and mediation practice but also opened the door for me to keep learning more about how and why humans behave as we do. They laid the groundwork for my happiness studies—and trained me to be a facilitator and presenter.

I have other favorite happiness teachers whom I have never met, including Sonja Lyubomirsky and Piero Ferrucci; my copies of their books are quite dog-earred with many sections underlined, highlighted, and starred. I have also greatly appreciated Barbara Fredrickson, Catherine O'Brien, and—definitely not least—the father of positive psychology, Martin Seligman.

More recently, the work of Sister Joan Chittister, Sherri Mitchell, and Margaret Wheatley have helped me understand the happiness movement within a broader spiritual and historical context. Their wisdom is priceless.

Some very important sources for me have been websites. BrainPickings.org overflows with rich and beautifully written insights and DailyGood.org provides inspirational news every day. *Greater Good Magazine*, published online by The Greater Good Science Center at UC Berkeley, should be bookmarked by every happiness student for regular access. And PsychologyToday.com is a consistently helpful resource in better understanding many human conditions.

The Greater Good site led me to two researchers whom I have particularly valued: Dr. Fred Luskin, an expert on forgiveness, and Dr. Robert Emmons, an expert on gratitude.

I am very much in debt to three Unitarian Universalist ministers who have been my role models: my sister, the Rev. Dr. Kathryn Ellis, Rev. Mara Dowdall, and Rev. Joan Javier-Duval. With no formal education on how to address a congregation from the pulpit, I have relied on studying what they do. I could ask for no better teachers.

Thanks, too, to the Worship and Arts Committee of the Unitarian Church of Montpelier for first inviting me to preach. I especially thank Ron Cameron, who guided and accompanied me through that experience with such grace and warmth.

I am grateful to every Unitarian Universalist church which has welcomed me to be their guest preacher. I am especially grateful to the First Universalist Church and Society of Barnard, Vermont, where every one of the sermons in this book was first delivered. Thank you all for your support; I am honored to serve you.

I must also acknowledge the Montpelier Ukulele Players, who have joined me for many a sermon and other GNH events. Ukulele music makes everything happier! They make me happy, for sure.

The Health Center in Plainfield, Vermont, gave me my first opportunity to teach meditation and mindfulness classes. Those classes were invaluable in deepening both my spirituality and my appreciation of these practices.

One special person in my life, massage therapist Kayla Becker, has also served as my counselor, life coach, and cheerleader for nearly twenty years. She has unfailingly believed in me. Truly, it is hard to imagine that I would ever have written even one sermon, much less a book of them, without Kayla's monthly dose of support. She's been a great gift.

Two other friends played a pivotal role: Anne Connor, who helped me reconnect with my writing self, and Jeff Mandell, who told me about the Certificate in Positive Psychology program. Their insights proved transformational in my life.

More recently, I've had the good fortune of connecting with the Rootstock Publishing team. From the start I have felt supported, understood, and respected. I am blessed to be working with people who share my values and respect my mission.

I am so appreciative of the love and support of friends and family, including my adult children Jennifer and Benjamin, and my now eight-year-old granddaughter Madeleine. While listening to one of my sermons is not Madeleine's idea of a good time, she is excited that her grandmother is publishing a book.

There are way too many friends to thank here, but Jeannette Cabanis-Brewin, Eva Centeno, Braco and Nevenka Probic, Ginger Clammer, and Bronwyn Fryer have all played important roles in helping me develop this book.

And one more shout out for my husband Bob. He is always there—as a ukulele player, the chief chef, my computer technician, on and on. Recently he has gone above and beyond by volunteering to help me with the endnotes. What a guy!

Finally, I say thank you, thank you, thank you to my brilliant editor, Amabel Kylee Síorghlas. I never understood why writers raved about their editors until I met Amabel. Now I get it! This book is so much better thanks to her insights, persistence, and big, big heart that loves planet earth and wants us all to do better.

May it be so.

Becoming a Happiness Preacher

I believe I've been striving for justice since I popped out of the womb. "That's just not fair," was one of my first rallying cries. Much to the amazement of older siblings, I protested parental discipline and lightning did not strike.

My earliest memory of political action was with some of those siblings, when I was six and John F. Kennedy won the Democratic nomination. We marched in circles upstairs chanting, "We want Kennedy!" while my brokenhearted parents, fans of Adlai Stevenson, watched the convention downstairs. Perhaps not excellent judgment on my part, but I've consistently fought for social justice ever since.

Maybe I was also destined to pursue joy. According to family lore, one afternoon when I was a toddler alone in the crib, my mother heard me making noises and came to see what I needed. Nothing, apparently: I was standing in the crib, rocking back and forth, cooing, "Happy, happy, happy, happy."

Naturally, I love that story, but maybe lots of babies do the same thing. Certainly, I was never the happy-go-lucky type. I wasn't the one grinning and acting goofy in old photos. In fact, it took me more than half a century to realize my happiness calling. If it was destiny, destiny took a long time to show up.

While it is not surprising that justice and joy have played a significant role in my life, there were definitely no early indicators that I would wind up as a part-time preacher. In fact, I only went to church as a kid on a handful of Girl Scout Sundays, which I both eagerly anticipated and dreaded. On the plus side, I got to wear my dress uniform, a sash full of badges, and, best of all, little white gloves. Solemnly, we carried our banners down the center aisle, a ritual I loved. On the other hand, my fellow Scouts all seemed to be Christians who went to church regularly. They knew what to do; I had no clue. As a middle child of six, I wanted to blend in. I was terrified of missteps. Fortunately, nothing embarrassing ever happened.

Once or twice, when I was visiting my Catholic grandmother and cousins in upstate New York, I went to Mass, an even more mysterious event. All I remember is that I had to drape a lace mantilla over my head. This was even better than the gloves! I didn't understand why I had to hide my hair, but no matter. I adored the mantilla.

There were a couple of summers when some of my siblings and I went to Vacation Bible School. Here's what mattered there: crafts and cookies. I liked that just fine.

When I grew older, I crossed the threshold of multiple churches for memorial services and weddings—the first of which was my own, in my husband's family's Lutheran church. Except for the groom, nothing about the wedding was what I would have chosen—but then again, I was seventeen years old, three months pregnant, and in a weak bargaining position. Spoiler alert: that groom and I will soon celebrate our 50th wedding anniversary, so that church visit turned out okay.

By my mid-thirties, with my children nearly grown, I felt stronger and more frequent spiritual yearnings. For what,

2

I didn't know. I dabbled in organized religion, including a handful of Quaker meetings and Unitarian Universalist services. I took up yoga and meditation. Once, I went to a weeklong yoga retreat that turned out to be a Hinduism intensive. Again, I loved the ritual: chanting, chocolate, flowers, candles, and incense. I loved the message and yoga and meditation, too. That retreat was so powerful, I semi-seriously contemplated the Hindu path—for about two weeks, until I decided I'm just too Western.

As my desire for a spiritual home grew, logistics got in the way. I was a full-time artist for thirteen years, spending Sunday mornings at craft shows, hustling to make sales of my hand-painted jewelry. No church for me!

Finally, in my early fifties, I abandoned the craft show scene for graduate school and a master's in mediation at nearby Woodbury College. Woodbury emphasized understanding one's own interpersonal relationships and conflict styles in order to be the calm eye of a mediation storm. The best way to recognize and control my personal conflict triggers (i.e. grow more mindful and compassionate) seemed to be to just go to church. Plus, my Sundays were now wide open! Despite a lack of white gloves, lace mantillas, chocolate, and incense, the Unitarian Church of Montpelier (UCM) was my first choice. In 2005, I walked through its impressive Civil War-era front doors for a standard Sunday service.

A friend had described Unitarian Universalist (UU) services as akin to drinking "decaffeinated coffee." Indeed, the UCM interior and lack of ritual was certainly spare compared to my Hindu experience. However, minister Maggie Rebman was very funny, smart, and inspiring. I returned several Sundays in a row and then joined the choir, which sealed the deal for me. I was on the other side of fifty, but I had finally found a spiritual home.

Turns out, there's nothing quite so uplifting as singing in a church choir, for so many reasons: community, learning, and drumming spiritual lyrics into your brain. Not that choir is easy for me. Rehearsal is often frustrating, exhausting, and very hard. I love to sing, and can occasionally hit a lovely note, but I'm not musically gifted. I don't even understand how anyone can keep time, stay on pitch, and sing the right words all at the same time! Nonetheless, choir became my community within a community, a place of belonging that helped my nervous, grown-up, middle-child self relax and be at ease with the larger congregation.

I officially joined UCM, and attended services regularly. Of course, the choir was usually singing, so I would have been there even if the sermons weren't generally quite wonderful, riveting even, under a succession of ministers. Maggie retired, and was replaced by the amazing Rev. Mara Dowdall, who later moved on to a bigger church and was replaced by another incredible minister, Joan Javier-Duval, who consistently makes getting out of bed early on Sunday mornings well worth the effort.

The idea that I might someday deliver a sermon myself first arose during Mara's tenure. I noticed that lay members of the church were, on occasion, guest preachers. Simultaneously, I began to have knowledge and ideas I wanted to share. I began to wonder if I might someday be invited to step into the UCM pulpit to preach about happiness.

I was delightfully surprised when the invitation did arrive, via email. I was on vacation in a backwoods cabin in Maine with my husband, my sister Kathy (a genuine, bona fide UU minister), and her husband. We had very spotty Internet service, but it was enough to send an immediate acceptance. I was fully committed to leading my first Sunday service. It was thrilling, and ... daunting.

Part of creating that service was choosing the hymns and "special music." Fortunately, my husband Bob is a key member of the Montpelier Ukulele Players. Since no music is happier than uke music, I asked Bob if he and the other Montpelier Players would be guest musicians at my guest service. They said yes, and a beautiful partnership was born. They've now become my "backup band" of sorts.

The ukulele music would set the mood and the choir would go all-out; however, I still had to write and deliver the morning's main event, the sermon. No pressure there. For so many reasons, I wanted that sermon to be really, really good. I wrote and rewrote, practiced aloud and rewrote again. I knew that many people considered happiness to be fluffy, and selfish. I wanted to make clear that cultivating personal happiness is one of the best things we can do to be of greater service to our troubled world. I wanted to be funny, poignant, compelling, meaningful and, god help me, not boring!

And ... it came together beautifully. That first sermon led to invitations from other area churches, and eventually to guest pulpit gigs as far away as South Carolina and Wisconsin. Turns out, even without the gloves and mantilla, I like church. I like listening, singing, and preaching. It makes me a happier, better person.

As for my own happiness, it didn't show up in a full-blown way until about my fifth career. In retrospect, I can see that the years leading up to my rendezvous with destiny provided me with the knowledge, strength, courage, skills, and insight to eventually teach the why's and how's of well-being, from the pulpit and elsewhere.

If one has nothing to say, or lacks the courage of one's convictions, it seems pointless to face a congregation or a roomful of workshop attendees. These people are looking for inspiration, education, and motivation. Learning to speak my truth is another clear memory that I carried from childhood.

I'd pinpoint the second grade when I was one of two in my class of twenty-four to choose John F. Kennedy over Richard Nixon in our mock election. It's not that anyone patted me on the back and said, "Good for you for standing up for your outside-the-norm beliefs." But neither did the world come tumbling down around me. I could safely be me.

However, it wasn't always safe and thus the need for courage. I wasn't safe at fourteen, in the emotionally perilous ninth grade, when I was one of a tiny handful of white girls who publicly had black boyfriends. To be clear, I didn't date interracially to be brave or make some kind of statement. I just wanted a boyfriend! I merely responded positively to the handsome boy who expressed interest in me.

This seemingly normal adolescent behavior incurred the wrath of strangers, a few teachers, and two of my best friends whose parents forbade them from associating with me. Sadly for them, the rest of our class rallied around me and they became exiles. This deepened my courage and, much later, compassion for those two exiled girls. The experience also gave me a slight understanding of racism, perhaps opening the door to an ongoing education about the ravages of white supremacy—something I think everyone who wants a happier world should face head-on.

The journey continued. I encountered lesson upon lesson through the years. With outspoken liberal parents in conservative central Pennsylvania, I was often out of step with cultural norms; I was a feminist and anti-war protestor by high school. But everything seemed to work out all right in the end. I was building resilience and a certain freedom to go my own way. I even had autographs in my yearbook that said things like, "To a girl who stood up for what she believed."

My first real job was writing copy for a public television station across the street from the Hershey chocolate factory. There I stood up for my truth (battling wage discrimination) and paid the heavy price of getting fired from my dream job of co-hosting a public affairs show. But the television heartbreak led directly to the best on-the-payroll job of my life: working in the communications department of Common Cause in Washington, DC.

So is the glass half empty or half full? I'm going with half full. Sometimes, yes, I've cried bucketloads of tears. Still, life has worked out pretty well. Common Cause, for example, was filled with smart, good people, all working hard for a better world. They inspired me then *and* now, as many of us have kept those sleeves rolled up for decades in a quest for the ideal in a realistic, down-to-earth way. The chairman of Common Cause at that time, Archibald Cox, remains my personal gold standard when questions of ethics or integrity arise. I need only ask myself, "What would Archie do?" to find my own best answer.

And yet, my journey was not over. I outgrew Common Cause professionally and moved on to a few other similar but less rewarding jobs. A few years later, I'd had enough and took another leap, joining the craft show world to display and sell my watercolor jewelry. This life chapter held many other lessons, including the rewards of creativity and entrepreneurship, as well as large dollops of humility and gratitude—two fundamental keys to a happy life. The gratitude wasn't about sales. Rather, with hundreds of strangers admiring my work every weekend, I simply had to learn to say thank you, and to mean it.

I loved making a living (meager though it was) from painting, but it, too, was not my calling. I was never an Artist with a capital "A." After I found myself crying in the bathroom during one of my formerly favorite craft shows, I knew it was time to go ... but where?

It was *still* not time for me to hear happiness calling. I had one more major growth phase ahead of me. But it wasn't just me—the world was not ready for the happiness movement either. In the Far East, Gross National Happiness was coming alive in tiny, isolated Bhutan. In the West, Martin Seligman, the University of Pennsylvania scholar who is widely considered to be the father of positive psychology, was working with his academic colleagues to give birth to the science of happiness. It would take a few years for these new ideas to ripen and spread.

Thus, I entered graduate school with no clue that my mediation studies were yet another building block to prepare me for teaching and preaching happiness. And prepare me they did! Among other things, my mediation training was a deep dive into the research and theories of human behavior, an endlessly compelling subject which is also at the heart of both individual and collective happiness.

Then there's conflict resolution itself, also necessary for happiness since our well-being depends on relationships and all relationships inevitably hit rocky shoals. Likely, that means we need to practice forgiveness, another rich area we explored at Woodbury College. Both grad school and my mediation work also taught me the value of leaning into the pain and life's hard choices as a way of moving forward productively. I became much more capable of, as one of my teachers put it, "leaning into the thorns."

My mediation career taught or refined the invaluable skill sets of writing, presenting, and listening—skills that I would need as a happiness advocate. After my final years working in Washington, DC, when I felt I was asked to use my words as weapons, I had completely shelved writing in favor of a paintbrush. Of necessity, I became a writer again in grad school. I also had no choice but to learn to stand in front of groups of people as a presenter or facilitator. While initially intimidating, growing comfortable in this role was incredibly important. After all, who wants a nervous preacher?

Of greatest value, though, was learning to listen. Every one of us comes to church or any other event in different life circumstances with various values, joys, hopes, and sorrows. It is important to me as a preacher to try my best to understand that, and to "listen" to everyone in the pews before me, even if all I can "hear" is their body language.

Finally, finally, I had my rendezvous with destiny. After spending my final months in grad school writing about mediation and suffering, I picked up Daniel Gilbert's *Stumbling on Happiness* and entered the brave new world of positive psychology. Gilbert is a great writer, and I found his hypothesis fascinating that we often don't make our own best happiness decisions. I was hooked on happiness.

A few months later, I casually bought a life-changing book in an airport: *The Geography of Bliss*, by Eric Weiner. Weiner describes his travels to some of the world's happiest countries, including Bhutan, the birthplace of Gross National Happiness. I was immediately *very* taken with the idea of using happiness and well-being as the framework for policymaking. It was love at first read. Just a few weeks later, Gross National Happiness (GNH) became a centerpiece of my life.

Perhaps it was coincidence, perhaps it was kismet. One spring day when I was walking the muddy dirt roads of my hometown, a stranger who was out for a run stopped to talk with me. Her name was Linda Wheatley. She had recently returned from the Third International Conference on Gross National Happiness in Bhutan, and she was determined to host a GNH conference in Vermont.

My reaction was, "Oh my god! I have got to be part of that! We are stopping at my house so I can give you my business card." Within weeks, as Linda and I sat around my kitchen table working to create a new organization, Gross National Happiness USA (GNHUSA), each of us pledged to the other, "This is it. This is my life's work."

So it has been. I entered the happiness movement through the systems change doorway—that is, the desire to work for major policy changes to improve lives from the top down. However, I quickly came to believe that personal transformation is also necessary to create momentum for desperately needed big picture changes from the bottom up. It's been a journey of personal growth and learning, as well as trial and error, in reaching out to others—*all* others, anybody and everybody I could get to hear or read me, anywhere I could find even the tiniest soapbox to stand on!

GNHUSA did indeed hold the first ever gross national happiness conference in the United States. It was called, "GNH2010: Changing What We Measure from Wealth to Well-Being." It was energizing and exciting, and I was totally hooked. Since then, I've been on and off the board, including a stint as president. I opened and closed my own "Happiness Paradigm Store and Experience." I've walked approximately three hundred miles in six states as part of GNHUSA's on-foot listening tour of the USA, the Happiness Walk. I've earned a

Certificate in Positive Psychology with Tal Ben-Shahar, created the Happiness Paradigm blog site, presented at conferences and events coast-to-coast (including Costa Rica!),
taught, coached, and led workshops.

And, I've preached happiness. I love the preaching format
because: a) people come to church *wanting* to hear what the
preacher has to say, and b) I believe the kinds of changes we
face require both knowledge and soul-searching in a loving
and supportive context.

Over the last decade, I have found in so many people
a hunger to understand happiness on a deeper level, both
for greater personal comfort and to be better citizens of the
world. That is what I try to offer with every service I have
the honor of leading and what I hope the reader will be able
to take away from the sermons in this book, no matter your
faith or lack thereof.

Each of the sermons in this book was delivered in a
Unitarian Universalist setting but they espouse no particular theology, other than "the gospel of happiness." In
particular, this collection of sermons was delivered over
three summers at the First Universalist Church and Society
of Barnard, Vermont, an historic, picturesque summers-
only gathering. To some extent, the sermons build on one
another, though the sermons can be read in any order, as
each addresses a specific aspect of individual and collective
well-being and happiness.

As you read, you might imagine me speaking from the
pulpit because each chapter was initially delivered orally.
I have a relatively soft voice, which many people have told
me they find pleasing. I am definitely no "booming author-
ity." One of my fellow sopranos told me, "A lot of times,
you look at the person in the pulpit and think, 'That's

easy for you to say, you're like an angel.' But you, Ginny, you're no angel."

It's true. I'm no angel, or guru, or even an academic superstar. I may have researched and studied the gross national happiness movement and positive psychology more than most, but I remain a soprano in the choir of life. On occasion, I hit some good notes. And, rehearsal is still challenging on a regular basis.

None of these sermons has all the information or all the answers you might wish to have. Sermons can only open the door, maybe nudge you on your journey—but it's your journey. This book may touch your heart or soul. It might ignite intellectual curiosity. But you have to find your own answers.

In her 2017 book, *Who Do We Choose to Be?: Facing Reality, Claiming Leadership, Restoring Sanity*, social scientist Margaret Wheatley (no relation to Linda Wheatley) writes unflinchingly of systems collapse and the need to create "islands of sanity." One key to these islands of sanity, she says, is treating people as *human* human beings.[1] Humans who need justice. Humans who deserve joy. I hope this book provides some of the inspiration and information to help co-create that justice and joy in your own corner of the world.

May it be so.

Happiness for Everyone: Our Moral Obligation to Change the Economic Paradigm

First Universalist Church and Society of Barnard
July 9, 2017

When the last tree is cut, the last fish is caught, and the last river is polluted; when to breathe the air is sickening, you will realize, too late, that wealth is not in bank accounts and you can't eat money.

—ALANIS OBOMSAWIN
"Conversations with North American Indians" in Who Is the Chairman of This Meeting? (1972)

My family was big into board games when I was growing up. A particular favorite was *The Game of Life*. After spinning the wheel of fortune, you got to steer a tiny car driven by your itsy-bitsy peg person over actual bridges next to 3-D buildings. It was thrilling to go to college, earn a degree (hopefully in a high paying field), get married, and gather pink and blue children to fill the family sedan.

In a way, it was a bit maudlin as we headed inexorably, though colorfully, toward our final reckoning—the end of life in this board game fantasy land. And who won the game? Of course, the player with the most money and material well-being. Not the one who had the most satisfying career, or gave generously in community service, or who had a car full of pink and blue loving family members. Nope. It was all about financial assets. That's how you win at life, board game-style.

Amazing to think back on it now. How well-trained we were to measure what matters in a real-life economy based on never-ending growth and consumption!

But life isn't actually a game with inflexible rules. We can make other choices. Indeed, it is a moral obligation for us to do better—for ourselves and others, including future generations—so we can all be genuinely and collectively happier.

That's what Greenpeace President Annie Leonard urges us to do. Before assuming her current role, she made provocative animated videos, like *The Story of Solutions*, which suggests we can move toward a happy, sustainable planet by redefining what winning looks like. Currently, Leonard says that our cultural end goal is *more*—more money, bigger yachts, shinier toys, more prisons, more polluting smokestacks, more, more, more. Instead, Leonard suggests, we need "simply" to change the goal of our collective lives to *better*.[1]

Though I hardly think it will be "simple" to switch from *more* to *better*, Leonard's solution is brilliant, for at least three reasons.

First, she neatly illustrates that "more" does not equal quality of life *at all*. The GDP barometer merely measures how much money changed hands. It is completely amoral.

That money could be—and mostly is—within the hands of a tiny fraction of humanity. It can include the costs of new solar panels, it's true, but it also includes money for new fossil fuel infrastructure. It *does not include* much that gladdens the human heart, such as our spiritual practices, trees, or grandbaby hugs. Despite the fact that the GDP was never meant to measure more than the exchange of goods and services, it's become the primary barometer for our collective well-being. It is high time we created a better barometer!

Second, Leonard provides a positive, common sense alternative. She never actually uses the words "gross national happiness," but that is essentially what she prescribes—a new, inclusive, holistic way of measuring and encouraging a life well lived by actively reframing what success looks like.

Finally, I find Leonard's solution brilliant because it is based on the very human hunger for accomplishment. Winning the game. This hunger can lead those who might push a little too fervently to overachieve. Taken too far, this drive might even manifest as greed. This is important, because some think that greed is at the heart of many societal ills and, certainly, the pursuit of an illusory infinitely growing economy.

But what if greed could be channeled as a social good? The work of Martin Seligman makes me believe this is possible. In his book *Flourish,* Seligman—who is not only viewed as the father of positive psychology, but is also the former head of the American Psychological Association—used the acronym PERMA to describe the five key "elements of well-being." The *P* stands for experiencing positive emotions, *E* for engagement using one's strengths, *R* for positive relationships, *M* for meaning, and *A* for accomplishment.[2] I find this grid helpful for understanding what motivates both individuals and societies.

Of the five happiness needs, it's the *A*, accomplishment, that is most unexpected and intriguing. While all of the measures can be used for darkness or light, accomplishment seems especially prone to amorality. Though it can mean inventing a life-saving vaccine, it can also mean razing the rain forest to build a golf resort.

Yet, the desire for accomplishment is a life force we can harness. Both *The Story of Solutions* and the Gross National Happiness movement take the aikido approach and work with, not against, human nature. Nobody's talking about utopia. We're envisioning better approaches that can be taken by real humans, with all their complex wiring, including the accomplishment drive which sometimes ramps up to all-out greed. By changing the end goal—what we want to achieve—to *better*, we can encourage everyone, including Type A overachievers and those in the grips of greed, to focus those desires directly on happiness rather than on the stepping stones of stuff and money.

One way to do that is to change what we measure.

As we wind our way through life, both personally and systemically, we use measurements to gauge how we're doing. It matters very much what we choose to measure, because that's where we focus our limited time and energy. Believe me, in that *Life* board game, which I always wanted to win, I paid careful attention to accruing financial assets.

In real life, you can measure the cash in your retirement accounts, your blood pressure, and/or how much fossil fuel you're burning—depending on your own narrative—and that data will guide your choices, to an extent at least, consciously or subconsciously. Yet, each data point represents a small fraction of your overall, complex story. To adequately assess your progress through life, you need a comprehensive, thoughtful set of measures. Perhaps you'd like to note how many friends you have dinner with regularly? Or the number of volunteer hours you put in? Maybe the mountains you've climbed? Or languages you speak?

One of my measurement tools is a pedometer. I'm one of those "10,000 steps a day" people. The steps are good, but the pedometer doesn't record whether I've taken the calcium I need for my osteoporosis, done my daily back exercises, meditated, had too much wine or eaten too much chocolate. It doesn't measure if I've gotten enough sleep, hugged anybody, or savored the sunset. So I have created my own scale—charts I fill in to note whether or not I've practiced gratitude, drank enough water, been nice to at least one person, and ... gotten in my 10,000 steps.

Measuring GDP is kind of like the pedometer gone haywire, measuring one thing and one thing only. Yet, there it is, regularly and enthusiastically cited in respected news sources: the GDP is up, or down. As if that alone tells us whether we're happy and whether we're well.

What the GDP tells us is to keep striving for more money, and then to go shopping, even though, as Buddhist writer Roger J. Corless put it, "trying to be happy by accumulating possessions is like trying to satisfy hunger by taping sandwiches all over your body."[3]

Anybody who thinks our rising GDP is making us collectively happy need only look at the 2017 report on suicide from the Centers for Disease Control. Celebrity suicides, often in the news, are just the tip of a very deep iceberg. The CDC found record-breaking levels of suicide in all age, gender, and socio-economic groups—including children.

Our GDP addiction also causes massive unhappiness worldwide. Scottish novelist Alexander McCall Smith, author of the *No. 1 Ladies Detective Agency* books, wrote poetically and piercingly about this. In *The Right Attitude to Rain*, Smith's fictional philosopher Isabel Dalhousie leads a discussion of "the lifeboat question." That is, if a ship is sinking and there are not enough lifeboats, how do you decide who to save? Smith writes:

> The focus moved on from real lifeboats ... to the earth as lifeboat. And here the issues became very much ones of the real world, Isabel thought, because real people did die every day, in very large numbers, because the resources of the lifeboat were not fairly distributed. And if we might feel squeamish about throwing a real and immediate person out of a real lifeboat, then we had fewer compunctions about doing those things which had exactly that effect, somewhere far off, on people whom we did not know and could not name. It was relentless and harrowing—but most of our luxuries were purchased at the expense of somebody's suffering and deprivation elsewhere.[4]

Then of course there is the effect of relentless economic growth on the planet itself. Many consider our current economic system to be the root cause of climate change and mass species extinction.

The GDP doesn't care.

However, a Gross National Happiness (GNH) system, with a goal of "better," does care. The GNH framework is holistic and comprehensive, using data from across the realms of human and planetary well-being. GNH adds in all the factors, such as how are we doing with income inequality? Are we in right relationship with nature? How successful are our education and health care systems? Do we have enough time to play and to enjoy life? GDP is in there too. It's just in proportion, like using the pedometer only as part of a well-rounded health measurement.

The country of Bhutan has been working on implementing GNH since 1972, when their king at the time told a reporter, "We do not believe in Gross National Product. Gross National Happiness is more important."[5] So in 2008, Bhutan, which is now a democracy, added this to their constitution: "The State shall strive to promote those conditions that will enable the pursuit of Gross National Happiness."[6]

Bhutan determined that there are nine key areas, or domains, of human well-being where governments, corporations, and other systems can enact policies supporting—or undermining—the pursuit of happiness.

These domains are psychological well-being; living standards; good governance; health; community vitality; education; cultural diversity and resilience; balanced time use; and ecological diversity. In other words, as a country they have a set of inclusive, holistic measures.

Major decisions are run through an extensive grid that measures multiple factors within *each domain* to determine if a particular law or policy is likely to increase or decrease the people's happiness. "Better" is absolutely the bottom line.

Gross National Happiness is still a young system and movement. The entrenched obstacles are significant, but GNH is spreading. Under the leadership of Prime Minister Jacinda Ardern, New Zealand, a country with a sophisticated Western economy, has adopted a well-being budgeting approach. Their finance minister Grant Robertson said in a press release, "We want a wellbeing focus to drive the decisions we make about Government policies and Budget initiatives. This means looking beyond traditional measures—such as GDP—to a wider set of indicators of success."[7]

The city of Santa Monica, California, has had a well-being project and a well-being city budget since 2014. Two states, Vermont and Maryland, have adopted Genuine Progress Indicators—a very watered-down version of GNH, but still, it's a start.

Even the United Arab Emirates has a Minister of Happiness. Countries worldwide recognize the urgency in UN Secretary-General Ban Ki-moon's message on happiness in 2014. He said:

> Happiness is neither a frivolity nor a luxury. It is a deep-seated yearning shared by all members of the human family. It should be denied to no-one and available to all. This aspiration is implicit in the pledge of the United Nations Charter to promote peace, justice, human rights, social progress and improved standards of life.
>
> Now is the time to convert this promise into concrete international and national action to eradicate poverty, promote social inclusion and inter-cultural harmony, ensure decent livelihoods, protect the environment and build institutions for good governance. These are the foundations for human happiness and well-being.[8]

The ideas aren't entirely new. Martin Luther King, Jr., for example, raised some of these questions in a 1967 speech to the Southern Christian Leadership Conference in Atlanta, Georgia:

One day we must ask the question, why are there forty million poor people in America? And when you begin to ask that question, you are raising questions about the economic system, about a broader distribution of wealth. When you ask that question, you begin to question the capitalistic economy. And I'm simply saying that more and more, we've got to begin to ask questions about the whole society.[9]

Imagine how a GNH system might work here. The most challenging part of implementing a happiness measurement system would likely be reaching consensus on the overall framework. That framework would be built using domains (those areas of life where policy can encourage well-being among the citizenry), as well as the many individual indicators within each domain. Imagine your personal well-being chart on a much bigger, more complex scale. Since the domains and indicators we choose to measure will guide our collective policy choices and behaviors, there will be a lot riding on getting the measurements right.

Still, once the framework is in place, it will take some of the sting out of policymaking, because the choices will rest less on ideology and more on data. With universal health care, for example, the question would be less about personally approving or disapproving of universal health care as an ideal and more about using the grid to determine if adopting universal health care would lead to greater or lesser levels of overall well-being.

This all might sound dry and bureaucratic, but the impact would be anything but. For example, on a local level—the school lunch penalty. Have you heard about this? Many schools nationwide deny access to the regular menu for kids whose parents have fallen behind in paying for lunch. They are given instead, in some cases, two slices of bread with a slice of processed cheese.

Under a gross national happiness framework which values education, good physical and mental health, community vitality and spirituality *along with* economic well-being—all areas that we could surely agree on—how could we possibly deny any child a nutritious meal at school?

It's not that this idea is new either, or unAmerican. Our second President, John Adams, said, "Government is instituted for the common good, for the protection, safety, prosperity and happiness of the people; and not for the profit, honor, or private interest of any one family, or class of men."[10]

If this is the sentiment of one of our founding fathers, why then in public policy today do we see such avarice and indifference to suffering?

As a possible partial answer, once again I look to positive psychology and that field's research on human nature—specifically, our incessant social comparison. Sonja Lyubomirsky, author of *The How of Happiness: A New Approach to Getting the Life You Want*, says social comparison is pernicious and invidious.[11] While this need to keep up with the Joneses can be helpful—if the Joneses are engaged in inspiring activity—it mostly leaves us feeling "less than" and desiring more.

As one of my favorite philosophers, Bruce Springsteen, puts it, "Poor man wanna be rich, rich man wanna be king, and the king ain't satisfied till he rules everything."[12]

I don't aspire to royalty, but I do stumble over social comparison. Though I've been trying to live the GNH way since 2010, pursuing *better* for myself and others, I still feel the pressure of material social comparison. An unpleasant indicator of just how deeply entrenched GDP social comparison is within my own brain arose when I was collecting data for our tax return. I got upset by how little I had earned in actual dollars. Fortunately, I've been bringing my husband Bob along with me on my GNH journey. He knew enough to gently chide me, "That is such GDP thinking." Which helped. Eventually.

If it's not easy for individuals to make this practical but very dramatic shift, it will undoubtedly be much, much harder for whole systems to change. Harder, but practical, doable, and necessary.

So where do we start?

Movements are made up of individuals, individuals with hearts—and that's where we can start. In our own hearts. Cultivating our own spiritual beings. Rewiring ourselves to appreciate, nurture, and model what truly matters in life.

A popular quote (sometimes attributed to the Dalai Lama, and here from John Green's book *Looking for Alaska*) says it all: "People were created to be loved. Things were created to be used. The reason why the world is in chaos, is because things are being loved and people are being used."[13]

Let's love people more, and things less.

Highly respected environmental activist Gus Speth, the former dean of Yale School of Forestry and Environmental Studies and part of Vermont Law School since 2010, suggests spirituality is key:

> I used to think that the top environmental prob-
> lems were biodiversity loss, ecosystem collapse
> and climate change. I thought that thirty years of
> good science could address these problems. I was
> wrong. The top environmental problems are self-

ishness, greed and apathy, and to deal with these we need a cultural and spiritual transformation ... and we lawyers and scientists don't know how to do that.[14]

Indeed, one of the best spokespeople for changing the economic paradigm is Pope Francis. After the terrorist attack in Paris, Pope Francis told reporters, "Terrorism grows when there is no other option, and as long as the world economy has at its center the god of money and not the person."[15]

No wonder, then, that the Pope says the economy must be:

> ... at the service of peoples. Human beings and nature must not be at the service of money. Let us say NO to an economy of exclusion and inequality, where money rules, rather than service. That economy kills. That economy excludes. That economy destroys Mother Earth.
>
> The economy should not be a mechanism for accumulating goods, but rather the proper administration of our common home. This entails a commitment to care for that home and to the fitting distribution of its goods among all.[16]

I'm not Catholic, but this still makes me say, amen!

Creating a just economy is clearly a deeply serious endeavor—but that doesn't mean we can't be joyful as we go about this work. Lord Richard Layard, co-editor of *The World Happiness Report* and Programme Director of Wellbeing at the London School of Economics, measures, analyzes, and ranks the happiness of individual countries.

He suggests we need to grow international happiness and sustainable well-being *together*. In other words, we need to talk about it. Layard thinks happiness clubs might be a good idea. I think happiness clubs sound delightful.

I also think we need to fall back in love with nature. As Gus Speth notes, "Materialism is toxic to happiness, and we are losing our connection to the natural world."[17] If we loved nature more fully, perhaps we would more determinedly include environmental concerns in our success measurements.

We can also cultivate the much-needed spiritual revolution by tending our own happiness gardens, which yields compassion for others, all others, even those far from our metaphorical lifeboats. Even those with whom we disagree. Even, miraculously, for our own flawed selves.

Let's redefine how we win at life. Let's swap *more* for *better*. Let's make happiness for all the new bottom line.

May it be so.

Happiness Runs in a Circular Motion

First Universalist Church and Society of Barnard
July 23, 2017

Even a happy life cannot be without a measure of darkness, and the word happy would lose its meaning if it were not balanced by sadness.
—Carl Jung
C.G. Jung Speaking (1987)

At a creativity retreat a few years ago, my friend Bronwyn grabbed her guitar and said, "Ginny, this should be your song." She then began serenading us with Donovan's song, "Happiness Runs." Bronwyn was onto something. The song's chorus which repeatedly asserts that "happiness runs in a circular motion"[1] seems prescient. The more I learn about happiness, the more I appreciate its circular nature.

The symbiotic relationship between personal well-being and a Gross National Happiness paradigm is a great example of the circular nature of happiness, though I'm pretty sure Donovan didn't have that in mind in the 1960s.

I also suspect that Donovan wasn't talking about the interdependence of happiness and sadness, though that connection is also necessary for good emotional health.

The circular motion between happiness and sadness is one that I've spent some time with lately. A little over a year ago, I developed troubling symptoms in my left eye—flashing, and a black spot, called a floater. Oh, yes, and just a *wee bit* of hemorrhaging behind the left retina. My optometrist sent me *immediately* to a retinal specialist.

There, on a gorgeous Friday afternoon in June, I learned that my vision was threatened by "retinal neovascularization"—bleeding behind the retina. I had already suffered some permanent loss of vision and would, without treatment, go blind in that eye *within a matter of months.* Doctor Kim told me I urgently needed to begin painful eye injections, starting the following Monday morning.

I was in shock. Permanent vision loss? Almost blind? Painful eye injections? What if the medicine didn't work? What if my right eye developed the same condition?

Over that long weekend, I unwittingly made the perfect happiness choice: I gave myself permission to dwell in sadness. To cry. To grieve. To acknowledge my mortality and fears about my very breakable body. I cocooned. I didn't want to be near anybody but my husband.

Fortunately, I rebounded pretty quickly, within the week. It helped that the eye injections weren't that painful, and that the doctor was reassuring about both my eyes and the efficacy of the medicine. It also helped that I've been building my happiness muscles for years now, and was better able to see many silver linings. Amazingly, the medicine is only ten years old. Before that, patients just went blind—so how lucky am I? Further, the symptoms that sent me to the optometrist were unrelated to the neovascularization. I am very fortunate that my vision loss was caught before it got any worse. Plus, I had health insurance. Can you imagine how much a retinal specialist costs? And brand new vision-saving drugs? Thank goodness I didn't have to go bankrupt to save my sight.

During this scary time, I posted a blog about my challenge and received a virtual outpouring of love and support from friends online. This filled my heart with joy.

Finally, I gained a valuable insight: happiness and sadness run in a circular motion. Paradoxically, happiness gave me the strength to grieve. Since I know what happiness feels like, and what I need to do to coax it back, I didn't need to shortchange the crying.

It works the other way around, too—that is, those who embrace the reality of suffering are better equipped to feel happy. We can't turn off the sad without also turning off the happy. As Golda Meir put it, "Those who do not know how to weep with their whole heart don't know how to laugh either."[2]

In Bhutan, where Gross National Happiness was born, they honor this belief in national policy. On a return trip to this happy country, *Geography of Bliss* author Eric Weiner found that the residents are encouraged to think about death five times a day.[3] That may be more than most Americans could handle. Nonetheless, I say, let's all have a good cry now and then. We'll laugh more later.

The circular relationship between sadness and happiness nicely illustrates that being your happiest self does not equate to a lifetime of sunny skies and smooth sailing. We are inescapably human, and fated to experience stormy seas. Trying to be happy when you really *need* to feel sad is a recipe for disappointment. That disappointment could feel like failure, thus creating deeper unhappiness. Not good.

The last thing I want to do is make anyone feel unhappy for not feeling happier! What I do want to do is share some of the why's and how's of cultivating happiness so you can recover more quickly from pain and live your best, most flourishing life.

What, then, is happiness? Because happiness is so personal, we all have different ideas of what it means. I think of happiness as contentment and peace of mind, with an enhanced capacity for joy, laughter, and other positive emotions. Researchers in the positive psychology field have used "flourishing," "thriving," and "positivity" as synonyms.

If happiness is a word that discomforts you, I invite you to translate what I'm saying to one of those words, or perhaps "well-being." It isn't the word that matters, it's the concept.

I definitely like the word *happiness*. Aristotle wrote, "Happiness is the meaning and purpose of life, the whole aim and end of human existence." *The whole aim and end of human existence.* I think that's pretty good. I'll stick with happiness.

In his groundbreaking book, *Authentic Happiness: Using the New Positive Psychology to Realize Your Potential for Lasting Fulfillment*, Martin Seligman says there are actually three levels of happiness:

- First is "the pleasant life" of savoring and appreciating basic pleasures such as companionship and the natural environment.

- Second is "the good life" which is achieved by discovering our unique virtues and strengths and using them to enhance our lives.

- Third is "the meaningful life," in which we find a deep sense of fulfillment by mobilizing our unique strengths for a purpose greater than ourselves.[4]

Seligman seems to build on the ancient Greeks who had two ways of categorizing happiness. First is Hedonic, or the pursuit of pleasure, which can include eating, drinking, sex, and pleasures of the mind and spirit. Second is Eudaimonic happiness, which comes from a life of virtue and excellence, with a sense of meaning, purpose, and concern for others.

Meaning comes up again and again as a crucial element of happiness, but pleasure is not to be scoffed at. We are biological creatures with physical needs and desires, which no doubt have important evolutionary tasks. Even if they don't, life is hard. Why not have joy and pleasure?

My primary positive psychology teacher, Tal Ben-Shahar, encouraged us to look at happiness as a blend of pleasure and meaning. He envisioned a quadrant with four choices:

- The first quadrant, with high meaning but low pleasure, is a rat race. Sometimes we need to live that way—for example, when starting a new and very demanding job, or caring for a dying loved one. It's grueling and not very happy to stay there permanently.

- The second quadrant, with high pleasure but little or no meaning, is hedonism. Though reveling in worry-free pleasure may feel good for a vacation, it can feel empty in the long run. If you doubt me, try it yourself. I just don't think any of us can go too long without doing *something* helpful.

- The third quadrant, no pleasure or meaning, is just plain bleak.

- Finally, the fourth quadrant is high meaning, high pleasure. That, says Ben-Shahar, is where happiness lives. Ideally, so do we.[5]

And yet, this isn't necessarily an easy formula to follow. For many of us—the fortunate ones not trapped in lives of desperate poverty, war, or other massive suffering well outside of our control—the pleasure-meaning balance is achievable most of the time. Even with our privilege, though, we are all likely to encounter dark episodes. When we are struggling with pain and grief, the last thing any of us should worry about is that we're not "doing happiness" well enough. Remember, the four-quadrant advice is a guideline, not a rule.

Also, it may be helpful to bear in mind that neither the pleasure nor the meaning have to be grandiose. The pleasure can come from a smile, a wildflower blooming in the sidewalk, or the reflections of a traffic light in a roadway puddle. Meaning can be as simple and as profound as basic human kindness.

The Dalai Lama has said, if you want others to be happy, practice compassion. If you want to be happy, practice compassion. One way to practice that compassion is to help move as many people as possible into that highly desirable fourth quadrant. We can do so by working for policies of social and ecological justice, maybe even as part of the GNH movement!

Here's something else the Dalai Lama wrote: in every single interaction with another person, we can either make that person happier, or less happy. Every. Single. Time. Given human nature and mirror neurons, that amazing part of our brain which automatically responds empathetically to what others are feeling, odds are good that they will likely respond in kind.

Kindness is not a panacea. Neither being patronizing, nor playing the martyr in the name of kindness will likely increase your own happiness. Still, as Ben-Shahar observes, "there is so much benefit to the person who gives that I often think there is no more selfish act than a generous act."[6] Indeed, the National Institutes of Health (NIH) found that giving money releases brain chemicals causing a "helper's high." Writer Nisha Jackson shares how Emory University research also found that the brain lights up with a helper's high, "a euphoric feeling, followed by a longer period of calm ... [and] a longer lasting period of improved emotional well-being and sense of self-worth."[7] So there you have it—the circular motion of kindness and happiness flowing back and forth between and among humans.

Aristotle, the Dalai Lama, and numerous sages and philosophers have been analyzing happiness for a long time. Even among Unitarian Universalists, happiness has been carefully considered. My sister, Rev. Dr. Kathryn Ellis, delivered a sermon on happiness that highlighted the teachings of Hosea Ballou, whom she termed "the foremost Universalist theologian of the nineteenth century."

Kathryn wrote, "Hosea was serene, calm, welcoming, affectionate, and well loved." She quoted his son as saying that Ballou "ever evinced an exuberance of good nature, and was amiable, gentle, and even playful at times."

Kathryn said, "Hosea Ballou believed that humans were motivated by seeking happiness ... and that God wanted people to be happy. Hosea Ballou flourished and wanted other people to flourish."

Now, modern scientists are taking the wisdom of these philosophers and religious leaders and subjecting happiness theory to scientific rigor. In the process, they are learning about what truly makes us happy, even on a physiological level, and the value of positive emotions in our troubled world.

Here is one of my favorites of their discoveries: all of us can be up to 40 percent happier.

Why 40 percent? You may have noticed that some people seem naturally happy. I always think of actor Michael J. Fox who, despite his debilitating Parkinson's disease, seems irrepressibly upbeat. Other people seem naturally unhappy, like they were born that way. Turns out, that's correct. We are all born with a genetic set point for happiness. When really good things happen, our happiness can soar. With bad events, our happiness sinks. But humans are remarkably adaptive, and after a bit, we return to our genetic set point.

However, scientists have determined that our genes only account for about 50 percent of our happiness. And they say that once our basic needs are met, only 10 percent of our happiness comes from the sorts of things we often think would make us happier, such as losing weight, getting a dream job or house, or exotic travels. In other words, the externals. That leaves 40 percent in our control—again, if we are privileged enough to not be in extreme poverty or war zones.[8]

We can build and maintain an enhanced happiness capacity through proven *and individualized* strategies, such as those detailed in Dr. Sonja Lyubomirsky's *How of Happiness* book. The cover features a meringue pie with about 40 percent missing to illustrate this point.

Quite recently, however, I saw an article in *Psychology Today* entitled, "Are You Ready to Take a Slice Out of the Happiness Pie?" This article discusses the research of Nick Brown from the University of Groningen in the Netherlands and Julia M. Rohrer from Leipzig University in Germany.

Brown and Rohrer dispute the 50-10-40 theory of how much happiness is within our own control.[9]

Their criticism is to be expected—that's how science works, constantly exploring, evolving, and questioning. Perhaps, as they suggest, the percentages are wrong. Further, they note, as I mentioned above in the happiness quadrant section, many individuals are in such difficult circumstances that making happier choices isn't a viable option. Brown and Rohrer also object to the idea of a "simple" happiness formula.

Yet even they say, "Finding your own fulfillment is certainly achievable, but to do so means understanding the complexities of the process." I agree. We humans are complex creatures. When it comes to our happiness, there are many options, distractions, misunderstandings, old habits to break, and new habits to break in. Nothing simple about it. The 50-10-40 formula may be off percentage-wise, but what matters is that with work and knowledge we *can* increase our happiness.

One way to do that is through rewiring our brains, which is also possible thanks to another interesting happiness theory I've learned about: *neuroplasticity*, which is the brain's ability to form new neural pathways and reorganize existing ones in response to stimuli.[10]

This is a bad news/good news story. The bad news: our brains are hardwired with a negativity bias that enabled us to survive in the Stone Age. The good news: our brains also retain their neuroplasticity pretty much until the day we die. That means, according to neuropsychologist Rick Hanson, we can literally rewire our brains for happiness by intentionally choosing to engage more frequently and more fully in positive thoughts and actions—both meaningful and pleasurable.[11]

Why does it matter? Staying on the happiness path will definitely help you achieve success, whatever that looks like to you. There's a myth that success leads to happiness; really, it's the other way around. Lyubomirsky and other researchers have found that happier people have more confidence, optimism, self-efficacy, likeability, sociability, and more originality. They are more active. Happier people also have better physical well-being, stronger immune systems, and more energy. And, happier people are more flexible and cope better with challenges and stress.[12]

Happiness is so good for our health that former United States Surgeon General Vivek Murthy made it part of his public health agenda. He emphasized happiness as one of the main ways humans can prevent disease and live a long, healthy life. He recommended strategies such as gratitude exercises, meditation, physical activity, and social connectedness, all of which boil down to another circular motion between mind and body.[13]

It seems that by taking care of the body, the brain will be happier. Murthy stressed exercise but sleep, touch, and eating well are also vital for happiness.

And a happier brain, in turn, leads to a healthier body.

Here's another circular motion that might be a bit unexpected: the well-being of animals and people is deeply interconnected. There are the obvious ways. Certainly pets make people happy, providing, as they do, both meaning and pleasure. But there are many other ways that animals increase our well-being, like bees that pollinate our food and bats that eat annoying insects. Not to mention cows and ice cream.

As for animals' well-being, my Gross National Happiness colleague Beth Allgood, United States Country Director for the International Fund for Animal Welfare, has done groundbreaking research on how our GDP-driven economy threatens the very existence of many species. If humans choose a Gross National Happiness path, the world's animals will be much happier too.[14]

There's another line from the Donovan song that speaks to many of these circular motions, and also seems so Unitarian: "Everybody is a part of everything anyway." This includes animals, other humans, even the trees around us. We are dependent on one another. In essence, we drink one another's sweat when it evaporates and then returns to earth as rain. We breathe the same air—even, literally, one another's breath.

Of course, happiness connections don't *always* run in a circular motion. Sometimes it's a linear path, such as actions which will have consequences down the line through time. Take children for example and the troubled world they may inherit from us. To address the issues we are passing along, we need to raise our children to be as happy as possible so they may be resilient and devise creative solutions. And to do that, says Christine Carter, author of *Raising Happiness*, we need to put on our own oxygen masks first. We need to walk the happiness talk for our children's sake as well as our own.[15]

Here's another linear happiness flow: from you, right now, to your future self. Rick Hanson says we have the most responsibility to those over whose lives we have the most power and that means ourselves.[16] Happiness is always a choice, one we make moment-to-moment. What do you think your future self would like you to choose?

Bronnie Ware, a palliative care nurse from New Zealand, essentially asked just that question in a research study. She asked her dying patients about regrets, and found five common themes. One of the five themes was, "I wish I had let myself be happier." She writes:

> Many did not realize until the end that happiness is a choice. They had stayed stuck in old patterns and habits. The so-called 'comfort' of familiarity overflowed into their emotions, as well as their physical lives. Fear of change had them pretending to others, and to their selves, that they were content. When deep within, they longed to laugh properly and have silliness in their life again.
>
> When you are on your deathbed, what others think of you is a long way from your mind. How wonderful to be able to let go and smile again, long before you are dying.[17]

Happiness is a choice. Through the years, many individuals (including B. Fay Mills who lectured on "The Happiness Habit" in 1911, in Racine, Wisconsin)[18] have been credited with saying some version of, "You can either mourn that the rose bush has thorns, or rejoice that the thorn bush has roses."

Whoever said it, I salute their wisdom. May we all choose rejoicing. May we all let ourselves be happy.

May it be so.

Growing Our Happiness Muscles to Build a Better World

First Universalist Church and Society of Barnard
August 6, 2017

Wherever we go, we can be a beacon of well-being, love, and care that not only touches but uplifts those whom we encounter.
—Jack Kornfield
"Why We Should Seek Happiness Even in Hard Times" in Greater Good Magazine (2019)

September 21, 2014, was one of the happiest days of my life. As I marched in the streets of New York City with roughly 450,000 other activists in the People's Climate March, I was awash with positive emotions. My heart was bursting with gratitude for everyone who showed up for what was, at the time, the largest ever call to climate action worldwide. I was proud to be there, too. The weather was perfect. All around me were music and chanting and vivid life, from babies to senior citizens with walkers—seemingly all races, genders, religions, and nationalities. There were scientists with an oversized chalkboard, a group from Minnesota with mini-windmills on their heads, and young adults dressed as fish on bicycles. We were in solidarity. We were hopeful.

Even waiting in the long, long lines for porta potties was an upbeat, connected experience.

It was an outstanding day.

Looking back, I realize that any number of happiness theories could explain why that day was a peak experience, and why, in many cases, activism makes us happier. In truth, standing up for justice is not always joyful in the moment. I've cried at anti-war marches, and at actions on behalf of children taken from their parents.

Activism provides meaning, deepens relationships, and, frequently, is carried out in a very positive manner. Not that I engage in activism to be happier. Indeed, I flip that equation on its head. That is, I firmly endorse cultivating personal well-being skills, in part, to help us be better activists.

In general, I believe in having a good time, and happiness theorists agree that pleasure is essential. As far as I know we only live one life. I am determined to make mine as happy as possible and I wish the same for you. At the same time, it is injustice, climate and otherwise, that spurs my passion and provides meaning. Together, this meaning and my determined happiness land me in Tal Ben-Shahar's fourth quadrant, a healthy combination of pleasure *and* meaning.

There is never a shortage of injustice, oppression, and other societal ills like addiction, loneliness, and income inequality. We each need to cultivate personal happiness precisely because the news and the heartbreak can otherwise overwhelm one's ability to effectively work for a better world. Happiness enables us to be those beacons of well-being and love, aptly noted by Jack Kornfield; happiness enables us to lift up others.[1]

Like most people I know, I have my down days, angry outbursts, hours of exhaustion, and crying jags. But none of us can afford to succumb to despair for too long. That's not an effective way to lead a life and not helpful to those who need the best from us *right now.*

While all of the happiness strategies in this book can help us to create a better world, in this sermon I want to focus on four ways to build our happiness muscles: utilizing the broaden-and-build theory, and cultivating our strengths, optimism, and resilience.

Broaden-and-build is the brainchild of researcher and social psychologist Barbara Fredrickson, whose credits include a stint as president of the International Positive Psychology Association, along with serving as Principal Investigator of the Positive Emotions and Psychophysiology Lab at the University of North Carolina, Chapel Hill. I had the good fortune of seeing Dr. Fredrickson at the 2016 Embodied Positive Psychology Summit. Fredrickson is so highly regarded, and so well liked, that she got a standing ovation *before* her presentation. She clearly walks the happiness talk.

One of the reasons Fredrickson enjoys such admiration in the positive psychology field is her groundbreaking "broaden-and-build" theory. Fredrickson notes that a negative frame of mind causes us to shut down somewhat, whereas, "Positivity opens us. The first core truth about positive emotions is that they open our hearts and minds, making us more receptive and creative."[2] That is broadening. The build aspect refers to our resources—physical, intellectual, and social—which help us to achieve our individual and collective best.

Fredrickson gives multiple examples of how broaden-and-build works in real life, including the cliché that "the family that plays together, stays together." This, she points out, is a good example, because the positive emotions of play help build the resources of family togetherness. Here's another of Fredrickson's examples: when you are interested in something or someone new, "your mindset is open and curious." In other words, broadened so you can better build your knowledge and understanding of the world.[3]

Imagine the many ways this can help us as activists! By broadening our mindsets via positive emotions, we can not only strengthen our group bonds and better understand the challenges we face, but also have more success in finding creative and doable solutions.

I've seen broaden-and-build at work in my mediation practice. Often when people begin the conflict resolution process, they are too angry to even imagine the possibility of a mutually satisfactory solution to their problems. As the mediation proceeds, the negative emotions are unpacked, people are heard, and understanding can begin to emerge, or broaden. This by no means happens in every mediation, but when more positivity does enter the room—in the form of hope, apology, and compassion—the ideas for building solutions also multiply.

Mediation is a nitty-gritty way of explaining broaden-and-build. I also like the lofty approach, which Fredrickson uses as the start of her chapter, "Broaden Your Mind" in her book *Positivity*—loftiness which comes from Rumi: *There is a way of breathing that's a shame and a suffocation and there's another way of expiring, a love breath, that lets you open infinitely.*

Aaahh, so lovely. Here's something else that's lovely: we can all bring our best selves to the never-ending task of making the world a better place by learning about our character strengths and putting them to work.

Positive psychologists have already done a lot of the work for us. Starting in the early 2000s, a group of fifty-five scientists, led by Martin Seligman and Christopher Peterson, spent several years classifying positive traits in humans across the globe. They found twenty-four universally admired virtues and strengths—or character strengths—which each of us has to one degree or another. A few examples are love of learning, humor, humility, forgiveness, and prudence. The VIA Institute on Character, founded by Seligman, Peterson, Mayerson, and others, explains that, "Character strengths are different than your other personal strengths, such as your unique skills, talents, interests and resources, because they reflect the 'real' you—who you are at your core."[4]

Among these twenty-four traits, there are a handful which will stand out for each person as *signature strengths*, the true essence of one's being. It's easy to find out what your signature strengths are because the VIA folks have created a free survey on their website that takes just a few minutes to complete. You then receive a ranked list of the twenty-four character strengths. The ones at the top are your signature strengths. The ones at the bottom, though, are *not* weaknesses. Prudence is generally near the bottom for me, but that doesn't mean it's a weakness—just not my strongest strength!

This is a feel-good exercise if ever there was one. Not only are there no wrong answers to this survey, but you can bask in reading how wonderful you are with all your outstanding strengths and virtues. Dr. Neal Mayerson, chairman of the VIA Institute on Character, spoke at the same conference where I saw Dr. Fredrickson. Mayerson said that these qualities represent the "incredible reservoir of wonderfulness that resides in us."[5] All of us.

Here are two other observations from Mayerson, which I put in my notes that day:

- Greater knowledge and use of our strengths will "tip humanity toward our better nature and increase human goodness."
- "Strengths don't make the dark part smaller, but greatly enlarge the good."

During the bad times you can use your signature strengths to get your own equilibrium back sooner and to be of greater service to others in pain. It only makes sense. Times of crises are the wrong times to try to behave like someone else. Far better to rely on your best authentic self.

In the year-long Certificate in Positive Psychology program that I completed, Dr. Maria Sirois led the unit on character strengths. She says, "Some strengths—core strengths—seem to be with us from the beginning … They simply are who we are." She notes that, "Self-esteem and competency both rise when we are in our highest strengths."[6]

Sirois advised us to keep a laminated copy of our signature strengths next to the bedside table, so when emergencies arose we could quickly choose our best response. Sirois also illustrated how our strengths can be helpful on ordinary days, recalling a time that she was inside Home Depot with two sullen teenagers waiting in the car, a cranky customer in front of her in the checkout line, someone grumbling in line behind her, and a frazzled store clerk. Sirois said she told herself, "Remember your strengths, Maria!" Since one of her core strengths is humor, she began telling jokes. Soon everyone around her was laughing and in a much better mood.[7]

It was just a moment in a checkout line, but why not make such moments more pleasant? It's good practice for the tougher challenges. Bringing our most authentic selves to the surface in daily life will carry over into our activism work as well—an arena where we definitely want to be our most effective, confident, and even happiest selves.

Here's something else you can do for yourself and those you wish to help: retrain your brain to be more optimistic. Before he became the father of positive psychology, Martin Seligman researched optimism, which he says is "invaluable for the meaningful life. With a firm belief in a positive future, you can throw yourself into the service of that which is larger than you."[8]

Right about now, I suspect most of you fall into one of three categories: 1) You already identify as an optimist, so you suspect this part of the sermon will reaffirm your beliefs; 2) You consider yourself a dyed-in-the-wool pessimist, and may feel skeptical about what I have to say next; or, 3) You consider yourself neither optimist nor pessimist but rather a realist, so are perhaps also a little skeptical.

Whichever category you fall in, you may wish to reconsider, because, as it turns out, nobody is born either an optimist or a pessimist. Seligman's research shows that optimism and pessimism are learned traits—and can be unlearned.[9] Being a realist isn't even a viable third choice, as reality can be appraised from anywhere on the optimism–pessimism spectrum.

I suspect some people choose the labels "realist" or "pessimist" because there's a misconception that optimism is disconnected from reality. That is not the kind of optimism I am talking about. I am advocating optimism that is firmly grounded in reality. Otherwise, it would be the kind of false positivity that Fredrickson cautions against. As Abraham Maslow put it, "False optimism sooner or later means disillusionment, anger, and hopelessness."[10] Whereas healthy optimism is literally good for our physical selves.[11]

That healthy optimism is available to all of us. In his book, *Learned Optimism: How to Change Your Mind and*

Your Life, Seligman explains the difference between pessimists and optimists, and why it matters:

> The defining characteristic of pessimists is that they tend to believe bad events will last a long time, will undermine everything they do, and are their own fault. The optimists, who are confronted with the same hard knocks of this world, think about misfortune in the opposite way. They tend to believe defeat is just a temporary setback, that its causes are confined to this one case. The optimists believe defeat is not their fault: Circumstances, bad luck, or other people brought it about. Such people are unfazed by defeat. Confronted by a bad situation, they perceive it as a challenge and try harder.[12]

An optimist, according to my teacher Tal Ben-Shahar, uses positive thinking in the form of high motivation, self-esteem, and the ability to interpret events in a constructive manner. He brought this theory to life with a metaphorical race in which both an optimist and a pessimist participate (I am paraphrasing Ben-Shahar's story).

The highly-motivated optimist overflowing with self-esteem might believe she will win. The pessimist thinks she'll only come in about tenth place. The race happens, and the pessimist comes in tenth, while the optimist comes in eleventh. What happens *after* the race is critical. The pessimist's goals of coming in tenth were met; no need to do more. The optimist interprets her loss constructively. She might think, I needed to train harder, or, I need better shoes. And then, with motivation and self-esteem fully restored, she tries again. And again. Eventually, success is within reach.

The optimist and pessimist may both reach their goals, it's just that the optimist sets the bar higher. You could say both were being realistic.[13]

Ben-Shahar also shared a story of Thomas Edison as a great example of optimism at work. When Edison was trying to invent the lightbulb, it took him a long time to succeed. His friends urged him to give up, noting that one thousand experiments had already failed. Interpreting events constructively, Edison said no—one thousand experiments had succeeded in proving what didn't work. It took him another thousand or so experiments, but eventually, he invented the lightbulb.[14]

Whatever our cause, we activists will inevitably lose many times, but grounded optimism can help us keep our cool, and press on. Admiral James Stockdale, the highest ranking naval officer to be held prisoner during the Vietnam War, illustrates this point with his observation that the POWs most likely to survive that experience were those with reality-based optimism. Conversely, the prisoners who thought they would be released almost immediately and the POWs who believed they would never be released did not survive as well.

Stockdale said, "You must never confuse faith that you will prevail in the end—which you cannot afford to lose—with the discipline to confront the most brutal facts of your current reality, whatever they may be."[15]

Here's another way optimism is helpful: it builds resilience. This point was trumpeted in the headline of an article in *The Atlantic:* "The Benefits of Optimism Are Real: Having a Positive Outlook Is the Most Important Predictor of Resilience," in which Emily Esfahani Smith wrote:

A positive outlook in difficult circumstances is not only an important predictor of resilience—how quickly people recover from adversity—but it is *the* most important predictor of it. People who are resilient tend to be more positive and optimistic compared to less-resilient folks; they are better able to regulate their emotions; and they are able to maintain their optimism through the most trying circumstances.[16]

Resilience is a word that gets bandied about so much these days, it seems almost trendy. Sometimes I wonder, what exactly makes resilience so special? But really, it's pretty fundamental. It is simply the capacity to rebound after adverse events. Perhaps it is special because life contains so many setbacks and pitfalls, on both the personal and collective levels. Resilience is invaluable in helping us move forward productively, and even happily.

Given the importance of resilience, it's great to know that this is a quality we can grow. Indeed, that's basically the title of psychologist Rick Hanson's 2018 book, *Resilient: How to Grow an Unshakable Core of Calm, Strength, and Happiness.* Hanson explains that:

Mental resources like determination, self-worth, and kindness are what make us *resilient*: able to cope with adversity and push through challenges in the pursuit of opportunity.... True resilience fosters well-being, an underlying sense of happiness, love, and peace. Remarkably, as you internalize experiences of well-being, that builds inner strengths which in turn make you more resilient.[17]

In other words, resilience supports happiness. Happiness also supports resilience—it's another beautiful, virtuous cycle. It just makes sense. When we know how to tune in to the positive in our lives, when we have built our personal resources, when we have confidence in our individual strengths, and a sense of grounded optimism, then of course we can bounce back faster from setbacks!

From that resilience can come hope, which is vital to moving forward. Howard Zinn notes:

> To be hopeful in bad times is based on the fact that human history is not only of cruelty, but also of compassion, sacrifice, courage, kindness. If we see only the worst, it destroys our capacity to do something. If we remember those times and places where people have behaved magnificently, this gives us the energy to act.[18]

Back at the People's Climate March in 2014, I saw thousands of people behaving magnificently. They seemed to be full of energy, hope, and kindness. Though it was only one day and one march, it lives on in my heart as a reminder of what activists can do when we are at our best. For our hurting world, may we be hopeful, may we be happy, and may we continue our fight for justice.

May it be so.

All You Need Is Love — But It's Complicated

First Universalist Church and Society of Barnard
August 27, 2017

Shared joy is a double joy; shared sorrow is half a sorrow.

—Swedish Proverb

In August 2017, my good friend Drew joined me at the Barnard church for the start of an eight-day visit. She had traveled from Washington, DC a few days earlier to visit with some New Hampshire friends, who then delivered her to Vermont to hear me preach. Drew and I have known each other for more than thirty years, since we first met in 1981. With such a long-standing relationship, Drew felt comfortable in telling me how she found one part of my sermon that day to be "dogmatic." That was the part when I said relationships are necessary to happiness.

I looked up dogmatic in the dictionary, since I was pretty sure—but not positive—that her concern was unwarranted. The dictionary says dogmatic is being "inclined to lay down principles as incontrovertibly true."[1] Perhaps I should have been clearer in my sermon that current research within the positive psychology field strongly indicates that we all need relationships to be happy. It may not be incontrovertible.

Still, plenty of researchers have weighed in on the topic. Social psychologist Daniel Gilbert, professor of psychology at Harvard University, asserts, "Social relationships are a powerful predictor of happiness—much more so than money."[2] And researchers Ed Diener and his son Robert Biswas-Diener, both giants in the positive psychology field, say, "We are prewired to make connections with others—relationships are necessary for our personal and physical well-being—and happiness is the grease that allows this emotional machinery to work."[3] In their research on extremely happy people, Diener and Seligman found that the one factor happy people had in common was close, supportive relationships.[4]

Perhaps the best example of the key role that relationships play comes from Dr. Robert Waldinger, director of the amazing 75-year-long Harvard study assessing happiness among adults. Waldinger says, "The clearest message that we get from this 75-year study is this: good relationships keep us happier and healthier."[5] *The clearest message ... is that good relationships are fundamental to health and happiness.

I have my own evidence, gathered during my participation in the Gross National Happiness USA qualitative research project: the Happiness Walk. After starting in Stowe, Vermont, in 2012, participants in the Happiness Walk (primarily Paula Francis, who walked much of the way solo) logged 10,000 miles in a loop around the United States before finishing in Boston on November 2, 2019. I myself only walked three hundred miles. Along the way, we happiness walkers asked anyone interested in talking with us—people of all ages, races, political views, and socio-economic circumstances—to go on record about what matters most in their lives.

The data from these interviews is being transcribed and analyzed; GNHUSA will release the results to great fanfare when complete. But those of us who've been on the walk know, without a doubt, what the number one answer was: relationships. Family, friends, and community. I have walked in and interviewed residents of suburban Philadelphia, northern Florida, the Acadian region of Louisiana, Santa Fe, New Mexico, and the Portland-Seattle corridor—five very different parts of our country. We got many different answers to our "what matters most" question. There were variations on the relationship theme, too, but nonetheless, everywhere and with everyone the clear, popular choice was relationships.

I am not sure if the GNHUSA study counts as rigorous scientific research, even if it does involve many thousands of interviews. Still, I think it's fair to note that our research, alongside that of the academicians and scientists, solidly supports the focus on relationships as being fundamentally important to happiness.

The value of quality relationships in our lives just makes good sense because, as philosopher Francis Bacon put it, "Friendship doubles joy and cuts grief in half."

Nonetheless, I should have expected Drew's reaction, or something like it from someone, in part because the term "relationship" might be assumed to mean having a romantic partner. Certainly that is one form, but as noted in an article in *Psychology Today*, "There are many other ways to love." Indeed, author Neel Burton, MD warns of a downside to that kind of limited focus. "By preoccupying ourselves with romantic love," he says, "we risk neglecting other types of love that are more readily accessible and may, especially in the long term, prove more healing and fulfilling."[6]

Burton then describes the seven types of love as defined in ancient Greece:

- Eros, a sexual or passionate love;

- Philia, or friendship;

- Storge, familial love, especially between parents and children;

- Agape—my personal favorite—the big, universal love;

- Ludus, which is playful;

- Pragma, a practical love based on reason, duty or long-term self-interest; and

- Philautia, or self-love.

So love and relationships come in many forms and stages. Yet no matter their form, relationships are undeniably complicated and a topic that can feel uneasy, especially for those in the midst of a deteriorating one. While relationships may be necessary for happiness, they can also be a source of much pain, sadness, and confusion.

To quote a modern sage from the august halls of Margaritaville: "Relationships! We all got 'em, we all want 'em. What do we do with them?" Jimmy Buffett, who cries this out in his "Fruitcakes" song,[7] notes in his own special way that yes, relationships may be challenging, but we want them anyway.

Because even worse is loneliness.

New York Times columnist Nicholas Kristof recently wrote that widespread loneliness is literally "killing us." He wrote, "Loneliness increases inflammation, heart disease, dementia and death rates ... but it also simply makes us heartsick and leaves us inhabiting an Edvard Munch canvas."[8]

This loneliness is heartbreakingly widespread. Kristof cites a 2018 Kaiser Family Foundation survey, which found that:

> More than a fifth of adults in the United States (22 percent) ... say they often or always feel lonely, feel that they lack companionship, feel left out, or feel isolated from others, and many of them say their loneliness has had a negative impact on various aspects of their life.[9]

Clearly, much more must be done to nurture healthy relationships, on both an individual and socictal level. Kristof reports that Britain has gone so far as to appoint a Minister for Loneliness.

While a lot of relationship wisdom is common sense, and much can be done on a personal level, positive psychology researchers and other scientists can offer us new insights and guidance.

One of those scientists is Dr. Fredrickson. After her broaden-and-build work, she went on to study the effects of love on human physiology. In the resulting book, *Love 2.0: How Our Supreme Emotion Affects Everything We Feel, Think, Do, and Become,* she writes that the relationships that make us happy don't necessarily need to be with other human beings. We can also have rewarding relationships with our pets. I know—saying that pets bring joy is stating the obvious. Still, science says it's so, and Fredrickson suspects that this is especially true with mammals because they are creatures that we can look in the eye and with whom we can not only give but receive love.

You see, Fredrickson is all about the physiology of love, and the health benefits of this vaunted emotion. When we make a loving, positive connection, even briefly, that makes us healthier.

This leads to helpful hint number two: such connections not only come from our furry friends, but also from strangers in what she calls "micro-moments" of love. Fredrickson writes:

> Love, as your body experiences it, is a micro-moment of connection shared with another. And decades of research now shows [sic] that love, seen as these micro-moments of positive connection, fortifies the connection between your brain and your heart and makes you healthier ... your micro-moments of love not only make you healthier, but being healthier also builds your capacity for love. Little by little, love begets love by improving your health. And health begets health by improving your capacity for love.[10]

I just love the micro-moment concept, and try to practice it regularly. On the Happiness Walk, we experienced frequent micro-moments of love, moments that seemed simply magical.

Maybe those moments were indeed magical. More practically speaking, I know that they were rooted in the connecting power of listening. On the walk, we listened with open minds and hearts to interviewees sharing their most closely held values. We weren't asking for money, or votes. We weren't proselytizing, or judging. We were *listening*. In turn, those to whom we listened felt safe in sharing amazing stories and poignant observations. The microbursts of love just exploded all around. Then we said goodbye and continued on our separate journeys, most likely healthier and happier from the exchange.

Some of those people, though, have never really left me.

And, you don't have to be on a Happiness Walk to listen deeply to others. Wherever you are, the results can be surprisingly touching. Profound, even.

Dr. Rachel Naomi Remen, an oncologist and author of *Kitchen Table Wisdom* says:

> The most basic and powerful way to connect to another person is to listen. Just listen. Perhaps the most important thing we ever give each other is our attention…. A loving silence often has far more power to heal and to connect than the most well-intentioned words.[11]

I have also seen the power of listening in my work as a mediator. In conflict, listening is especially important, because it's extremely difficult to hear your opponent's concerns when you yourself are not being heard. When people are heard, they soften, they begin to listen, and they open to possibilities.

We were taught the art of "active" listening in mediator training, which, by the way, was an emotionally challenging experience. Many of us cried, especially during role-plays. I'll never forget the day I was sobbing but still had to step into the mediator's chair for a role-play. I couldn't imagine how I could mediate when I was such an emotional wreck myself. The priceless advice I received was, "Just listen with all your heart." I did, and it worked. It almost always works. Like magic.

Just listen with all your heart.

It's a simple prescriptive, yet as observed by Stephen Covey, author of *The 7 Habits of Highly Effective People,* "Most people do not listen with the intent to understand; they listen with the intent to reply."[12] I've noticed that those replies often come in the form of unasked-for advice, or "issue hijacking," as in: "Oh yeah? Think that's bad? Well listen to what happened to me!"

Of course, none of us can be a good listener 24–7. That would not be happy making! We ourselves also need to be heard. Plus, active listening can be exhausting. Still, when the time is right, listen with all your heart. Even to babies.

I bring up babies because of a conversation I had with my friend Drew, who reminded me that relationships can help us be our best throughout the life cycle—from birth through death.

Drew and I were reminiscing about the year and a half when my daughter, a new single mom, came with her infant daughter to live with me and my husband Bob. It was an intense time and a lot of work, providing daily evidence that relationships are not always easy, and that times of great meaning in our lives may leave little room for anything other than the task at hand. However, our sacrifices were well worth the effort. Today, Bob and I can watch our happy, healthy seven-year-old granddaughter and know that we played a critical role in building the foundation she needed to flourish. Her happiness makes us happy, too.

The loving care we pour into relationships doesn't always pay off quite so evidently, but Drew reminded me of another time that had similar results—when Bob and I were brand new parents ourselves. I was seventeen and he was eighteen when our daughter Jennifer was born. Obviously, we needed a great deal of help to get her life off to a good start, and to get our own lives on track as well. Fortunately, we received a lot of help from our families.

Micro-moments of love are great, but throughout our lives we all need long-term, committed relationships to cope with raising children, getting an education, and navigating illnesses, losses and deaths, along with countless other joys and sorrows.

Indeed, relationships are at the very heart of a meaningful life. Sometimes we are the receivers, sometimes the givers. The rewards may be immediately clear, or never visible. Nurturing relationships can be pleasurable, challenging, or just kind of a drag. In the National Public Radio series, "This I Believe," essayist Deirdre Sullivan wrote:

> "Always go to the funeral" means that I have to do the right thing when I really, really don't feel like it. I have to remind myself of it when I could make some small gesture, but I really don't want to. I'm talking about those things that represent only inconvenience to me, but the world to the other guy. You know, the painfully unattended birthday party. The hospital visit during happy hour. The shiva call for one of my ex's uncles. In my humdrum life, the daily battle hasn't been good versus evil. It's hardly so epic. Most days, my real battle is doing good versus doing nothing.[13]

I, too, battle with showing up—fighting off the inertia of inconvenience to do the right thing. Yet often when I get there, I am so glad I came. Even at funerals there is a kind of pleasure because they not only "cut grief in half," they also build community. As we come together to share our grief and support the departed's family with casseroles and deviled eggs, we also nurture the communal relationships so vital to everyone's well-being. It feels good.

Showing up is an investment. According to my teacher, Tal Ben-Shahar, investing in relationships is one of the four key actions that healthy relationships need.[14] He urges us to invest time and effort in relationships, which will help ensure that others will be there to share our joys and sorrows. One day, we will all be the grieving loved ones in need of casseroles and deviled eggs.

Most of our relationship investments are not just one-offs. There are never-ending opportunities to invest—to pitch-in and cheer on. Or, to accept the help and good cheer. Last winter, for example, my husband invested all of February and half of March babysitting our granddaughter in Wisconsin while our daughter worked overtime. As for me, back on the Vermont home front, I was on the receiving end as friends made the effort to make sure I had enough firewood, a bedroom heater that worked, and companionship at dinner.

Here are the other three relationship actions Ben-Shahar advises: Allow for conflict, take time for joy and giving, and know and be known.

Ben-Shahar's second relationship prescription, to allow for conflict, is not an easy pill to swallow. In the short term, conflict often makes our brains and hearts unhappy, and who wants that? Yet as a mediator I can tell you two things you probably already know. One, conflict is inevitable. Two, conflict when productively handled can deepen and strengthen relationships. In turn, stronger relationships increase our happiness.

I can also tell you, even as a trained mediator who knows the benefits of conflict, I still shy away from it. Conflict is hard, no matter how you approach it. This is a big, messy, yet hopeful topic, more than enough for an entire sermon. Indeed, conflict is the theme of Chapter Seven.

Ben-Shahar's third relationship action, joy and giving, is a much more appealing step to take. This is another common sense observation supported by science. Sociologist Dr. John Gottman of The Gottman Institute has studied what communications are most likely to predict divorce and has concluded that healthy relationships should have five positive communications for every one negative interaction.[15]

Yet, how many of us frequently unload our frustrations and negativity on those closest to us? I have certainly been guilty of unleashing my pent-up stresses on my husband and children. Now, I try not to as much. And guess what? I have discovered that this is another example of happiness running in a circular motion! The more positive we are with our loved ones, the more likely they are to be positive with us. Joy begets joy.

Ben-Shahar's prescription, "know and be known," makes sense in terms of Maslow's hierarchy of human needs, which places the need for esteem and recognition near the top of the pyramid. We need to be known in order to warrant authentic recognition. I find it to be a real privilege to get to know others on a more soulful level, often over many years. And I feel emotionally safest with those who know me best. In their company, I feel free to just be me. Not only that, but when we really know someone deeply, we know how best to contribute to their health and happiness, and vice versa.

In these tumultuous times, another aspect of the knowing process that seems especially valuable is its capacity to help us understand the intricacies of the world better, therefore enabling us to act more in accordance with our values. I've been remembering a way that my dear high school friend Carlton let himself be known to me. Fifteen years ago, Carlton, then a PhD tenured professor at a major university, told me that every single morning he looks in the mirror and says, "You're a black man today. You're going to be a black man all day long."

It's taken me many years to even partially grasp the meaning of Carlton's morning ritual. What I believe he was allowing me to see is that the threat of racism is omnipresent. It's far worse than an occasional incident. As he continues to let himself be known to me, our friendship grows closer. And I am better able to understand white privilege.

Just as we construct ideas of who and what others are, we do the same with ourselves. If we believe we are good people, we need to behave that way—whether it's standing up to white supremacy or going to the funeral—or our brains will be unhappy with us.

Of course, despite the many, many benefits of relationships, Drew had a point that day, because love is not *all* we need. On the Happiness Walk in northern Florida, a teenager working in a convenience store wisely said, what matters most in life is air, food, and water. Point taken. Yes, we need more than love to survive.

And yet, another part of the Happiness Walk provided a memorable example of how prioritizing relationships can contribute to happiness. We were in the Acadian part of Louisiana, including Lafayette, which had recently been named the Happiest City in America by researchers from Harvard and the University of Vancouver.[16]

I wondered why. Turns out, Lafayette has some very serious problems. The city is near Cancer Alley, and cancer seems especially prevalent. Lafayette's main industry is oil processing, which was struggling at the time of our visit. One of our hosts was a human resources director who said she had to lay people off every day.

And yet, wow, was Lafayette a happy place! I concluded there were three main reasons: one, a strong emphasis on regular parties with extended family and close friends; two, exceptionally good food; and three, music. Gathering folks together sometimes for days on end for parties, food, and music seems like an excellent recipe for nurturing happy relationships.

Did I mention the food? Oh my, the best I've ever had. Another host told us about living in Lafayette, "If we're not eating, we're planning our next meal."

Obviously, cultivating strong relationships doesn't have to be hard work. Doubling the joy, cutting the sorrow in half—and having a good time.

Or, as our Lafayette friends put it, "Laissez les bon temps rouler." Let the good times roll. So much joy and sorrow to share *together*, creating a happier, healthier life for all.

May it be so.

Mindfulness and Compassion: The Foundations of Happiness

First Universalist Church and Society of Barnard
July 8, 2018

Seeking happiness outside ourselves is like
waiting for sunshine in a cave facing north.
—TIBETAN SAYING

Four years ago, deep into a frigid March night, I became acutely aware that meditation really does build greater compassion in ordinary people like me.

I'm a big believer in scientifically valid happiness research conducted by academics. Yet there are times, like that cold dark night when I would rather have been sleeping, when personal evidence seems to be equally valid research.

Before I go on, I must emphasize that my husband Bob is not, by any stretch of the imagination, a drunkard. What happened that night was an aberration, and a story I would not share publicly unless it was okay with him. It is, so here goes.

I had gone to bed early that night because I needed to be at my best the next morning. I was leading my second service at my home church, the Unitarian Church of Montpelier, or UCM for short. Bob also was making a repeat appearance at UCM as one of the leaders of the Montpelier Ukulele Players. They had rehearsed their songs. They were ready. Bob, however, had a major social commitment on this particular night—attending the annual neighborhood "Scotch Slop" for men only.

Since the "Slop" involves tasting lots of whiskey, I was worried that Bob would get drunk. Still, I wanted him to go to the party, because it is a community event he values. He promised to take it easy and be home early.

Around midnight, I woke up. No Bob. And no chance of me going back to sleep either, even though he got home shortly thereafter at 12:30 am.

I asked, "How drunk are you?"

He cheerfully responded, "Preeeettttty drunk!" And promptly fell asleep.

As the rest of the night progressed, I tossed and turned in my own bed, then on the sofa, and finally in the guest room where I had an epiphany: I was very upset at losing so much sleep, but I wasn't mad at Bob. At all.

This was a lightning bolt moment for me because I knew, beyond a shadow of a doubt, that before I had a regular meditation practice, I would have been furious with him while lying there awake in the dark. Fair or not, I would have been royally pissed off.

Instead, I felt compassion. Compassion for my husband, who had gone to the Scotch Slop for a rare opportunity to bond with other neighborhood men. Compassion for the other men, too, such good guys, well deserving of one night a year to drink alcohol together. Finally, compassion for myself, for not getting the sleep I needed.

I was amazed. I didn't feel like a different person, but part of me was definitely transformed. For the better.

I share this story for two reasons. First, I believe that meditating has actually rewired and possibly even restructured my brain to become more compassionate and less reactive. Current research indicates that a regular meditation practice may literally change our brains in three ways: by shrinking the reactive amygdala, a small but powerful part of the brain which triggers the "fight or flight" response; by increasing the size of the "temporo parietal junction, or TPJ, which is associated with perspective taking, empathy and compassion;"[1] and, thanks to neuroplasticity, by rewiring our brains to make compassion more habitual.[2]

That absolutely amazes me. We can *change our brains* through meditation!

The second reason I wanted to tell you about my compassion "aha!" moment is because we seem to be in a particularly challenging moment of history. America is bitterly divided over core issues. Democracy seems to be unraveling. Record levels of income inequality are creating dystopic differences between rich and poor. And environmental destruction and climate change hover over us all as an incomprehensible threat.

However, Reverend Susan Frederick-Gray, President of the Unitarian Universalist Association, has noted that it is not just "these times;" it is in *all times*[3] that suffering and injustice run rampant.

But these are *our* times, times that are crying out for all of us to be our most compassionate selves—for our own aching hearts, for each other, and for the broader communities with whom we are interdependent. If meditation and mindfulness are tools to increase our compassion, there has never been a better time to put them to good use.

You may be wondering, what is the relationship between

meditation and mindfulness? I'll explain the difference in a few minutes. But first, let me cite just a few more examples of how fundamentally important both are to personal and collective happiness.

In her seminal book *The How of Happiness*, researcher Sonja Lyubomirsky wrote:

> An avalanche of studies has shown that meditation has multiple positive effects on a person's happiness and positive emotions, on physiology, stress, cognitive abilities, and physical health, as well as on other harder-to-assess attributes like 'self-actualization' and moral maturity.[4]

Lyubomirsky says she would be skeptical, but empirical data is persuasive.

I was also impressed in 2015 when the Surgeon General at the time, Vivek Murthy, included meditation in his United States public health agenda. Murthy said that meditation, along with gratitude and social connection, "creates a greater sense of emotional well being, which then gives [people] the fuel and the energy, if you will, to go out and make changes in their lives and in their community."[5]

In my own work as a happiness teacher and writer, I've come to realize that mindfulness is a vital component of effectively developing almost any other happiness skill, such as curbing social comparisons, growing empathy and kindness, or appreciating the interconnectedness between animal and human well-being. In his beautiful and profound book on kindness, Italian psychotherapist Piero Ferrucci observes that mindfulness "is the medium through which kindness can flow. No attention, no kindness."[6]

Mindfulness impacts both self-awareness and awareness of others. How can you appreciate your role in creating and solving a dispute, in coming to forgiveness, without mindfulness? Awareness, by helping us to notice the
many positives in our lives, fosters gratitude, another key
to happiness.

So let's explore a little more deeply, starting with the
clarification of meditation and mindfulness. Tal Ben-Shahar
uses a helpful exercise metaphor to illustrate the relationship: You work out at the gym, yes—*and* you can also
exercise in many other ways and places. Shoveling snow.
Mowing the lawn with a push mower. Mopping the floor.
Exercise is frequently available to us, even without formally
working out.[7]

The same is true for the connection between meditation
and mindfulness. Taking the time to actually meditate is like
going to the gym. Just as you have options for which equipment to use at the gym, you have many meditation choices.
You can try watching your breath or your thoughts, reciting
a mantra, doing a body scan, or focusing on loving kindness.
Different forms of meditation offer different benefits, in addition to enhanced mindfulness, like greater body awareness or
more positive constructs of other people. The key elements of
all approaches to meditation are some form of attention or
intention, AND conscious deep breathing, all carried out in a
non-judging way. We're not aiming for perfection. It's called
a "practice" for a reason.

Certainly, meditation is a way to practice mindfulness, but
it is not one hundred percent necessary for living mindfully.
You can build mindfulness through a variety of activities, such
as being present and aware while you do the dishes, noting
the color and movement of the bubbles as they float on the

water, the squeak of your rubber gloves on a plate. Or while hiking, notice what your arms and hips are doing while your feet step forward. Is there a breeze, or is the forest utterly still? Maybe you could listen to music mindfully, rather than relegating it to background noise, letting the notes wash over you, perceiving their color, pitch, and patterns. Whatever activity you are engaged in, doing it mindfully is usually an option. Mindfulness can be a way of being.

Harvard social psychologist Ellen Langer, who has done intriguing work on the power of the mind to make measurable differences in the physical body, says mindfulness is "the very simple act of actively noticing things."[8] If you want to be mindful, just pay attention. What you notice could be within you. What emotions can you pinpoint? Maybe you feel some twinges or tired muscles. Are you feeling fatigued in general, or is caffeine racing through your bloodstream? You can also notice what surrounds you: the play of light and dark on the kitchen floor, the subtle sounds your house makes, or maybe the aroma of wood smoke on a cold day. Day after day, you may begin to notice changes within yourself, as well as in the environment and people around you. Meditation not required.

Well ... you can *try* to "just pay attention," but it is not easy. At all. Human minds are very busy places. The world around us is overflowing with distractions. I find it much more helpful to carve out peaceful meditation time, when I can gradually slow down the "monkey mind" to be more present and build my capacity to be attentive. I like meditating. It's a refuge.

While I appreciate Langer's work, I am more drawn to Matthieu Ricard, the Dalai Lama's French interpreter. In his book, *Happiness: A Guide to Developing Life's Most*

Important Skill, Ricard offers a poetic, happy view of mindfulness:

> It is a sparkling experience of inner well-being, in which the beauty of each thing shines through. It is knowing how to enjoy the present moment, the willingness to nurture altruism and serenity and to bring the best part of ourselves to mature—transforming oneself to better transform the world.[9]

Transforming ourselves to better transform the world. THAT is why mindfulness matters so much to me. Yes, there is a wealth of evidence that mindfulness can make us physically healthier, do better in school, be more creative, or have lower blood pressure. All good. But what I care about most is that becoming more mindful can make us better people. More compassionate. Less judgmental. Better equipped to serve.

Jon Kabat-Zinn, internationally known for his Mindfulness Based Stress Reduction classes, says, "Mindfulness means paying attention in a particular way: on purpose, in the present moment, and nonjudgmentally. This kind of attention nurtures greater awareness, clarity, and acceptance of present-moment reality."[10]

In my secular meditation and mindfulness classes, I teach that mindfulness means paying attention to what's happening within you and around you, and then, to illustrate, I share this story from a Jack Kornfield interview. Kornfield, a decades-long leader in the meditation movement, relates the true story of a military man with a serious anger management problem.

The superiors of the man in the story send him to a mindfulness training. When he returns, he naturally feels better. But then one afternoon in a grocery store he finds himself getting agitated toward the woman in front of him in line. You see, the woman has only one item but is in the regular line. She also has a baby, and she and the clerk are oohing and aahing over the child instead of tending strictly to business. The man grows angrier. Then, the woman hands the baby to the clerk and the military man nearly erupts.

Fortunately, his mindfulness training kicks in just in time. He recognizes his emotions and calms himself down. When it is his turn with the clerk, he says, "That was a cute baby." And she says, "Do you think so? That's my baby." She explains that she works at the grocery store because her husband was killed in Afghanistan. She tells him that the woman with the baby is her mother, who brings the child in to see her once during every shift.[11]

Thank goodness for mindfulness! Imagine if the man had exploded and dumped his toxicity on the two women. They would have suffered additional pain for no good reason. And he, likely, would have felt bad afterwards, instead of learning the clerk's story.

You may be familiar with the quote, "Be kind, for everyone you meet is fighting a hard battle you know nothing about." It is attributed to many different authors, including Plato. Whoever said or wrote it first, this is a very mindful practice. It requires being aware of your own emotions, as well as being sensitive to what's going on around you while withholding incomplete, useless, or possibly even destructive judgment. In essence, the definition of compassion.

Of course, mindfulness is not a panacea. Some of my students tell me they have become much more compassionate and less judgmental, but even so, they sometimes run into someone who really rubs them the wrong way. I know the feeling!

And sometimes we don't want to be mindful. But even that can be a mindful decision. When a wrenching audio clip was released of migrant babies wailing inconsolably in detention centers, I forced myself to listen to it. It seemed important to hear their pain. At the same time, an activist friend of mine made the opposite decision, choosing not to listen to their cries.

These are important choices, because we can't take it all in or take on all the battles. I have been working for climate change for many years, but I limit what new climate devastation news I read or watch. I don't want to be paralyzed with despair. We need to be compassionate toward ourselves and mindful of our capacity.

In the summer 2018 edition of *UU World*, Trudi Frazel uses the metaphor of a scuba diver for mindfully monitoring how we're doing. "Scuba divers use oxygen tanks to help them survive in the sea," Frazel writes. "They must carefully check their equipment before their expeditions, consistently monitor their remaining oxygen levels, and take action to get themselves to safety before they run out of the air they need to survive."[12]

Frazel suggests using this mindful approach in our daily lives—noting when our own oxygen supplies are on empty by listening to body, heart, and spirit. I imagine most of you can identify with her observation, "When I am nearly out of reserves, I need to act. I cannot continue to be an effective helper to others if I have nothing left in my tank."

No one can be mindful all the time. We're only human. Not only that, but it's helpful to our creativity to sometimes indulge in flat-out mindlessness. So no judging for all the millions of times our minds wander elsewhere.

One more thing: mindfulness can be enormously pleasurable, adding immeasurably to our quality of life if we just take the time to appreciate the many miracles around us. Think for a moment about the joys of a hot shower. Or the awesome beauty of puffy clouds in a cerulean blue autumn sky.

Or pillows and blankets. Have you ever taken the time to truly appreciate the softness and warmth of sinking into your own bed night after night? It's a gift you can re-open time and again, through the blessing that is mindfulness.

As Jon Kabat-Zinn says, mindfulness "is the direct opposite of taking life for granted."[13]

In possibly the best mindfulness essay ever, "Three Days to See," Helen Keller's words transformed my life. Frequently, when I find my mind wandering, or lost in painful thoughts, I remember this essay. Then I stop, and try to be truly aware of the world around me. Keller wrote:

> I who am blind can give one hint to those who see.... Use your eyes as if tomorrow you would be stricken blind.... Hear the music of voices, the song of a bird, the mighty strains of an orchestra, as if you would be stricken deaf tomorrow. Touch each object you want to touch as if tomorrow your tactile sense would fail. Smell the perfume of flowers, taste with relish each morsel, as if tomorrow you could never smell and taste again. Make the most of every sense; glory in all the facets of pleasure and beauty which the world reveals to you through the several means of contact which nature provides. But of all the senses, I am sure that sight must be the most delightful.[14]

Sometimes, I have to make myself be mindful. Other times, just as compassion can show up automatically, more expansive mindfulness is an easy companion. That's how it was one summer day when mindfulness helped me to truly see the needles of a scraggly pine tree by the side of a dirt road. For the first time, I noticed that the needles are *all* in sets of three, and that each of the three are different shades of green! Imagine, all these years I've been glancing at the same type of evergreens but seeing only one color of green, with zero awareness of the growth pattern of the needles. This is the kind of amazing, abundant discovery which can be ours for the taking, enriching our lives, if only we take the time to pay attention.

Becoming more mindful and thus more compassionate offers us another gift: the awareness that "this, too, shall pass," along with an understanding that most situations aren't as bad as our over-reactive amygdalas would have us believe. So it was, that cold night before my second sermon in the UCM pulpit. Thank goodness I didn't waste too much energy on being furious at my drunk husband, because the next day in church, all was well. His performance was fine, and so was mine. We were both able to be fully present, without being stuck in thoughts about the previous night or what we might say to each other later. Instead, we could both just be happy—preaching happiness and playing happy music— instead of wallowing in a marital dispute.

Not that I can always tap into compassion, or mindfulness. It's a lifelong practice, not a final product. The breath is always there so that the opportunity for mindfulness is always there. Breath by breath, and day by day.

May it be so.

You Don't Have to Be the Mermaid: Social Comparison and Empathy

First Universalist Church and Society of Barnard
July 15, 2018

*Happiness is found when you stop comparing
yourself to other people.*

—Anonymous

Back in my craft show days, I had plenty of opportunities to make myself unhappy by comparing my art and sales with other exhibitors. Often, I was surrounded by artists of a much higher caliber. If I had plenty of attention from my own customers, with their compliments and checkbooks, then I could happily admire the more talented artists and salespeople. If, however, the show was "slow"—our euphemism for few lookers and even fewer buyers—it was easy to see myself as a mediocre artist, an inferior salesperson, and possibly even a less worthy human being. Or, I could boost my fragile ego by looking down on those whose work seemed less skilled than mine, or those who had even fewer customers than me.

Neither option was very happy-making.

One memorable evening, though, I caught myself in active social comparison with the *customers*. I was at an opening night gala for well-heeled patrons. There was champagne, and goodies like mushroom caps stuffed with crabmeat—for the patrons, not for us. We exhibitors were specifically prohibited from helping ourselves to the refreshments. It was humiliating, and I resented the paying guests that night for having so much more money than I had. I saw them as a monolith, the "other," not as individuals worthy of compassion.

I had a friend with a nearby booth that night. She was also uncomfortable with the set up. She told me she felt like a mermaid—a mermaid who swims around in a giant indoor pool, visible to partygoers on the other side of a glass wall. A silent mermaid, on display, who doesn't partake of the mushroom caps or champagne.

That made me laugh, but also gave me pause. In a moment of clarity for which I have been forever grateful, I thought: *Wait a minute! What do I want or need in life that I don't have? What do these patrons have that I don't?* I had work that I loved. I was making a meager but satisfying living as a watercolor painter. I had a house I loved, very modest, but peaceful and pleasant. I was healthy. I had a loving partner and children who had grown up to be kind people. I had good friends, too. I was incredibly fortunate. There was no reason to feel bad by comparing myself to these unknown, dressed-up people. I could appreciate what *I* had, and not worry about what *they* had.

And then, with that realization: I was happy.

I'm forever grateful for such clarity, because I've returned to that moment over and over. At the time, I knew nothing about social comparison; I now know that it is one of the major barriers to personal happiness, especially for me. I can be kind, grateful, mindful—no problem! But releasing the grip of social comparison is on ongoing struggle. To combat that internal pressure, I often remind myself: I don't have to be that metaphorical mermaid.

And neither do you. Social comparison is so ingrained in our brains, we may not even be aware we are doing it. We may not realize the harm it can cause. It can be much more destructive than resenting someone else for eating stuffed mushroom caps. With awareness, we can diminish how much we constantly measure ourselves as compared to others, our striving to "keep up with the Joneses" so to speak. We may never be entirely successful—it is always a temptation to size up our houses, cars, body types, jobs, and children's achievements against those of our friends and neighbors, or even strangers in magazines. Yet we can quiet these incessant internal comparisons and even choose to ignore them.

That would, of course, be a good practice, because when we consistently feel inadequate, we make ourselves miserable. What a waste of our time and energy! Even worse, comparison often leads us to individually and collectively snub, judge, demonize, and even do violence to others. Social comparison can cause *a lot* of unhappiness and pain.

An oversimplified happiness cliché which contains a great deal of truth about comparison comes from Rabbi Hyman Schachtel, credited with saying, "Happiness is not having what you want. It is wanting what you have."[1] We need to be careful, however. The night I first chose to not be a mermaid, I had an abundant life. That is not always the case for everybody. Schachtel's statement is not as appropriate when it comes to serious deprivation, like going hungry so you can pay for medications. Wanting what we have can be tied to privilege. Certainly, being mindful about avoiding social comparison is internal work, but a homeless individual could hardly be blamed for comparing her housing situation with those living in cozy houses. Happiness is not just an inside job!

For those of us in more comfortable situations, we would be well served to appreciate our own good fortunes. Yes, someone else will always go on a better vacation or land a higher-paying, more exciting job. But why should that make us less happy?

Now this may surprise you: even with all its foibles, social comparison does have some positive aspects. First, wanting what we don't have—let's say, wanting to be a registered nurse—can be helpful in urging us toward goals we haven't yet attained.

Second, we can be positively inspired by others. For example, I've been very impressed with the courage of friends who have engaged in civil disobedience on behalf of the environment, the families separated at the border, and other social justice causes. I hope to someday have the same courage and commitment. Social comparison, yes, but in a good way.

Third, comparison with those who have less than we do can also be helpful, as long we're not gloating, preening, or taking pleasure in another's suffering. Rather, when we empathize with another's challenging situation, being mindful of and grateful for our own good fortunes, we can reduce our cravings for *more* and maybe, if possible, even reach out to help.

Let's take a moment, now, to define social comparison more fully. According to an article in *Psychology Today*:

> Social comparison theory states that individuals
> determine their own social and personal worth

based on how they stack up against others they perceive as somehow faring better or worse.... As a result, humans constantly evaluate themselves, and others, across domains such as attractiveness, wealth, intelligence, and success.... These evaluations can promote judgmental, biased, and overly competitive or superior attitudes.[2]

Because it's so ubiquitous, social comparison can persistently and perniciously undermine happiness. In *The How of Happiness*, Sonja Lyubomirsky warns, "People who pay too much attention to social comparisons find themselves chronically vulnerable, threatened, and insecure."[3]

Honestly, social comparison is a tough one for me. Maybe I need to meditate more, or maybe it's because I'm an animal. Dr. Loretta G. Breuning explains:

We cause ourselves pain when we compare ourselves to others. So why do we keep doing it? Because all animals compare themselves to others, and we've inherited the brain that creates this impulse.... Animals are always checking each other out. Their survival depends on it, and their brain chemicals respond with life-or-death feelings. We have the same brain chemicals and they give you the feeling that your life is threatened when you see someone with bigger antlers.[4]

Breuning acknowledges, "The curse of social comparison is hard to escape." Don't I know it! However, she says we all have the power to stop it. And how do we stop it? By being mindful, appreciating our own blessings in life, and accepting the reality that we all have strengths and shortcomings. Nobody and no life is perfect. Let's just get on with life as it is. Patience is also helpful here. With time and perseverance, we can all rewire our brains.

If we want to be happier, we have to exercise that power. Lyubomirsky's research confirms this need. "The happiest people take pleasure in other people's successes and show concern in the face of others' failures," she writes. On the other hand, "A typically unhappy person ... is deflated rather than delighted about his peers' accomplishments and triumphs and ... is relieved rather than sympathetic in the face of his peers' failures and undoings."[5]

Here's another unfortunate twist to how social comparison can sabotage our well-being: we are more likely to feel triggered by a *loved one* out-achieving us than by a stranger's success. *New York Times* "Smarter Living" editor Tim Herrera notes:

> We instinctively compare ourselves more to people who are close to us, even though, paradoxically, it can engender bitterness.... In fact, our brains are so bent on those comparisons that in one experiment, subjects *actively sabotaged* their friends from succeeding.[6]

The subjects didn't even realize that's what they were doing! Not a pretty picture. However, social comparison has even worse ramifications for collective well-being. It is clearly one of the key triggers that advertisers use to drive the consumer economy. I did a quick online search of "Social Comparison and Advertising." Google responded with six hundred three *million* results.

Shopping may sometimes provide a short-term happiness hit, but the *Journal of Happiness Studies* reports, "Americans have a lot of stuff, but are not necessarily happier for it ... even if we want what we have, we want more."[7] That's especially disheartening, given that many consider out-of-control consumerism to be a primary cause of climate change, environmental degradation, and species extinction.

There's even more bad news. On his *Hidden Brain* podcast, Shankar Vedantam explores social comparison in an episode entitled, "Feeding the Green-Eyed Monster: What Happens When Envy Turns Ugly."

Vedantam starts gently enough, citing the positive aspects of social comparison, but he soon gets down to business. "Everyone," he says, "at some time or another, will experience this feeling of wanting what someone else has, and resenting them for having it.... But envy can also turn malicious, prompting us to resentment, rage, and a desire for revenge."[8]

In the podcast, Vedantam cites numerous experts, including University of Kentucky social psychologist Richard Smith. Vedantam relates Smith's chilling view:

> But Richard says it could also be an act of cutting down of an envied group. In fact, he believes that malicious envy and schadenfreude may have been one of the underlying triggers of the Holocaust. The suffering of Jews in the 1930s and 1940s came after a time of Jewish prosperity when many average Germans were struggling financially.

It is an extreme understatement to note that social comparison taken too far can be very, very dangerous. Indeed,

Vedantam also shares this contemporary warning from Smith: "[S]chadenfreude has become a powerful force in our politics, and it operates through the lens of partisanship."

In the current highly partisan atmosphere, this is a deeply disquieting statement. Schadenfreude, which means deriving pleasure from the misfortunes of others, is no way to conduct our affairs.

But remember, on an individual level, social comparison is a choice—once we understand it and have the awareness to better recognize what is going on inside our own heads. Then we can choose a more constructive approach. In the *New York Times* article I quoted earlier, Vedantam, who also hosts the *Hidden Brain* podcast, explains:

> You can train yourself to recognize the symptoms when you exhibit them…. Say, for example, your best friend earns an award in your shared field … celebrate your friend's accomplishment—studies have shown that a loved one's accomplishment can even rub off on you, increasing your own self-evaluation.[9]

In other words, try empathy.

Empathy is described as the ability to understand and share the feelings of another. Actress Meryl Streep says, "The great gift of human beings is that we all have empathy; we can all sense a mysterious connection to each other."[10] Another extraordinary woman, Maya Angelou, concurs. She once said, "I think we all have empathy. We may not have enough courage to display it."[11]

Jeremy Rivkin, an economic and social theorist, and an expert on empathy, thinks that emotion may hold the key to our collective survival. So we'd better find the courage Maya Angelou talked about! Rivkin echoes Streep, believing we all have a capacity for empathy. In a 2010 animated video called *The Empathic Civilization*, Rivkin says, "We're actually soft-wired to experience another's plight as if we're experiencing it ourselves."[12]

You all know what this feels like. I've been watching silly cat videos with my granddaughter, and there's one where a cat knocks a large object on its owner's head. I wince every time. Thanks to mirror neurons, we've all cringed, shuddered, and sighed at the movies, and in real life, too.

I think it's important to note, empathy also means feeling good about the *joy* of others. There are things I still want and am unlikely to ever have, like, say, a lakefront house. Or things I want again but which are forever gone to me, like my youth. Social comparison might have me resenting those who currently possess what I want, but with empathy, I can choose to feel happy for them instead.

The question is not whether we have empathy, but whether we will use it. Research shows that we can increase our empathy if we're motivated to do so. Not everyone is. More power and more wealth seem to lead to less empathy. And, distressingly, our children are growing less empathetic. One study showed that modern college students are 40 percent less empathetic than earlier generations.[13] Forty percent. Wow.

We need to step in now and address this, especially on behalf of future generations. This planet needs more empathy, not less. To start increasing empathy, I suggest small but doable changes in our own lives.

Here's one very immediate, concrete practice you can undertake. Think about your reactions to your friends' good fortunes. Choose empathy over negative social comparison. See what happens.

You can do this even on Facebook. Some research is finding that Facebook increases social comparison, because everyone else's sanitized posts look so darned good! But Facebook is also a great venue for practicing empathy. Celebrate your friends' victories and joys—even if it's a fabulous vacation you wish you were on! Wish them well and observe how this makes you feel.

Empathy and social comparison aren't always directly intertwined. Sometimes empathy is about recognizing what you're doing and making other choices like gratitude. Of course, this is the kind of self-awareness and awareness of others that can come from—you guessed it—a meditation or mindfulness practice.

Here's another helpful exercise. Try writing down a list of all you do have, and are. You may be amazed at your abundance!

You can also just talk about it. I'm not sure how many people even know about social comparison. I don't think it had ever crossed my mind as a meaningful issue until 2010, when I first read Lyubomirsky's book. You can help to educate others.

You don't have to be an expert, and you can treat the topic with humor. Last summer, one of the Montpelier Ukulele Players showed my husband Bob his new ukulele socks. Bob joked, "Uh-oh, now I'm social-comparing." I love it! What a great way to spread awareness.

Ben-Shahar used to tell his students that we have "permission to be human."[14] Part of being human is being an animal, with social comparison as part of our basic biology, a survival technique. So no need for guilt, but also no free pass either. We have the capacity to triumph over social comparison urges, to be more empathetic, and to get along. To be, as Gandhi urged us, the change we want to see in the world.

May it be so.

The Road to Happiness Includes Frequent Stops in Conflict Land

First Universalist Church and Society of Barnard
July 22, 2018

Difficulties are meant to rouse, not discourage.
The human spirit is to grow strong by conflict.
—WILLIAM ELLERY CHANNING
Boston (1838)

The idea of becoming a mediator came to me in a mysterious way, as a gift from the universe. I was sitting alone in a cafe in Stockholm after having toured the Nobel Prize Museum across the street. As you can imagine, the museum was very inspiring. I was in a state of awe, along with wondering what to do with my own life, when the word "mediator" jumped into my head.

I was in Stockholm visiting a friend who worked at the US Embassy. Right before my trip, I had broken down in tears as I finally recognized that I no longer wanted to be a full-time artist. I had no idea what to do next, and was hopeful that I might find an answer in a foreign land, far from home.

Indeed, in that café, I knew immediately that mediation should be my next career. Within days of my return home to Vermont, I contacted the admissions office of nearby Woodbury College and began the process of enrolling in their Mediation and Applied Conflict Studies master's program.

It was quite a leap, especially since I didn't even know what mediation was. I had a vague idea that it was some kind of peacemaking process and involved working directly with people. That sounded promising; though, as I told the admissions counselor, I didn't like conflict. I hoped I could be a mediator who didn't have to deal with conflict. The admissions counselor, who became a close friend, later told me that my wish to avoid conflict made her believe I definitely would not follow through with the enrollment process.

But I did. I followed through in a big way, learning not only how to mediate in the midst of some very intense conflicts, but also how to coach new mediation students and lead conflict resolution workshops. While I still don't like conflict, I now appreciate that conflict resolution—though often distressing and uncomfortable in the short-term—can sometimes lead to richer relationships and greater happiness for the long-term.

My educated view of conflict is cautiously optimistic. The Dalai Lama says:

> Optimism doesn't mean that you are blind to the reality of the situation. It means that you remain motivated to seek a solution to whatever problems arise. Optimism involves looking at a situation not only in relation to problems that arise, but also seeking out some benefit—looking at it in terms of its potential positive outcome.[1]

Graduate school taught me that lesson. When the parties involved in a conflict are motivated to find a solution to their problems, positive outcomes are definitely *possible*. But there are no guarantees, and often the parties stuck in a seemingly intractable conflict don't feel especially optimistic. Nonetheless, productive conflict resolution can help steer everyone toward a better ending.

Graduate school is also where I fell in love with conflict *theory*. It was so cool to learn more about what is going on inside our very human hearts and brains during difficult interactions. Then, just days after finishing my mediation program, I picked up my first happiness book and also fell in love with the science of happiness. Fortunately, the two fields are inextricably connected, as happiness depends on having strong, healthy relationships, and healthy relationships remain vibrant and grow deeper through successful conflict resolution.

While conflict is inevitable, it need not be *frequent*. Previous chapters have already covered tips from positive psychology on ways to avoid unnecessary or unnecessarily harsh clashes: compassion for self and others, listening, mindfulness of what's happening internally and externally, and stepping back from social comparison. When disputes do arise, Fredrickson's broaden-and-build theory can help us find better solutions, and grounded optimism can lead the way to the light at the end of the conflict tunnel.

Conflict resolution theories, much like happiness teachings, hold true not only for an individual's one-on-one relationships, but apply all the way up to complex multinational conflicts. I have immense respect for mediators in seemingly intractable wars. My work is more intimate, with a focus on the personal, rather than group conflict.

At all levels, we would do well to heed Martin Luther King, Jr.'s advice: "Man must evolve for all human conflict a method which rejects revenge, aggression, and retaliation. The foundation of such a method is love."[2]

Love might not be the first word that springs to mind when we find ourselves in a conflict. But it seems clear that we need to be loving in conflict. If we want others to be happy, as well as ourselves, we need not only love, but to be brave, optimistic, and skilled in order to minimize the damage we might otherwise intentionally or unintentionally inflict.

Sometimes, we don't even need another person to get into a conflict. We can do it all by ourselves. Years ago, I went to a powerful weekend-long forgiveness workshop led by the spiritual writer and teacher Stephen Levine. He asked us to imagine an internal conversation about ice cream. The chatter might go something like this: "I really want that ice cream!" "No, no, I didn't exercise enough today. I don't deserve it." "Sure I do! I'll just have that one ice cream cone, and I'll exercise more tomorrow." Back and forth until you finally eat the ice cream. Which tastes great.

Then, the chatter turns quickly to, "Why did you do that? What is wrong with you?" And the guilt kicks in. That example resonates all too well with me. Internally, I frequently play out this very conversation, but now I do it mindfully.

For all of us, the ice cream example illustrates how easy it is to become enmeshed in conflict with self or others. It doesn't take much. Fortunately, heeding the wisdom of experts in the conflict resolution field can help us handle such situations more compassionately and constructively—not foolproof, but better. And happier.

One of the most well-known mediation experts is Ken Cloke, Director of the Center for Dispute Resolution in

Southern California. He says that in conflict the brain "feels assaulted and responds in a primitive manner, without realizing that what we are basically confronting is a lack of skill." He explains:

> The very first skill that we need to learn ... is a very simple one: Are we going to engage in the conflict and behave badly, or are we going to try to stop and figure out what's actually going on here? ... And the question then becomes, how do we exactly handle this? We often handle it through the passage of time. We get upset, stroll off, cry or pout ... whatever it is, but time passes and we return to a non-conflict state. Without having learned very much except, perhaps, to count to ten.[3]

This is why I love conflict theory. It shines a light on what really *is* going on, based on how we are wired and in each culture how we are trained to behave in conflict. Understanding what lies at the heart of a conflict, in turn, can help us to calm down and feel less assaulted. We can then make informed choices that are more likely to resolve the conflict, thus providing the possibility for personal and relational growth.

One of my favorite conflict resolution ideas is the concept that we all have rule books in our heads telling us what's right and wrong. It's a favorite because it makes so much sense, and is relatively easy to apply to real-life situations. Here's how the rule books relate to conflict: nobody's rule book is the same. The rules vary for your siblings, parents, children, partner, and best friends. Each set of rules is built by unique life experiences, and thus the rules we each play by while in conflict are uniquely our own.

I learned this lesson through a memorable exercise in graduate school. The instructor pretended to invite us to dinner at 6:00 pm on a Friday evening. We each wrote down the time we planned to arrive. When we shared our answers, the times ranged from 5:45 to 7:00 pm! And everyone had specific rules for their choices. The 5:45 people—two women from the Midwest—said, you have to arrive early to help. The 7:00 pm woman, from Manhattan, explained that arriving any earlier would be rude. The hostess might still be in her bathrobe!

The exercise was fun, and enlightening. It showed how readily conflict can arise because someone breaks one of the rules in somebody else's book. Even more importantly, I realized that we have a choice whether to make an issue over the rule infraction, or just let it go. Does this rule really matter? Sometimes rules matter, obviously. A simple rule that matters is that children should not chase a ball into the street in front of an oncoming car. Other times, you may decide that your rules don't need to always rule the situation. It's your choice.

On more than one occasion, I've caught myself flaring up about one of my broken rules that actually isn't that big of a deal. This helps my brain to calm down and feel less assaulted. You don't have to be a mediator—this is a practice anyone can try. My husband Bob, for example, has a rule that men don't wear hats indoors, especially in a church or restaurant. His hat rule came from his father's stern admonishments on the topic when Bob was a child. As an adult, on more than one occasion, Bob has gotten grumpy about men wearing hats in restaurants until he understood that it was his rule, not theirs. And, it isn't anything worth getting upset about.

The funny thing about this rule is that Bob's own father started wearing baseball caps inside restaurants during his final years! Sometimes, we not only let the infractions go, but say goodbye to the rules themselves.

On the other side of the equation, we've probably all been in situations where we've inadvertently upset someone else and didn't know why the other person was so irked. When that happens to me, if I'm able to take a breath and say to myself, "Ah ... I must have broken their rule about that," then I can react compassionately rather than combatively.

In contrast, I remember an incident that happened years ago when some friends and I got yelled at in a restaurant by a fellow customer for taking the next available table. We were next in line, so that seemed the reasonable thing to do, but something triggered this person, who had apparently finished her own meal and was on her way out. She voiced her strong opinions about how dreadfully we had behaved. She then stormed off, leaving us stunned and frustrated. I reacted angrily, with a resentment I carried internally *for years*. In retrospect, I wonder, what rule did we break? It could have saved me years of holding onto a grudge against that stranger if I had known about our individual rule books, and thus had a better way of framing her outburst.

Much more challenging than rules, though, and even more helpful to be aware of, are two powerful, built-in human tendencies. The first is attribution, which is a tendency to immediately judge others without necessarily knowing what is going on. The second is having a self-serving bias, which skews our self-judgment in a personally favorable way.

Of the two tendencies, psychologist Jonathan Haidt says that our failure to see ourselves more clearly—the self-serving bias—is the bigger problem. He quotes the Bible (Matt. 7:3-5):

"Why do you see the speck in your neighbor's eye, but do not notice the log in your own eye?" He also shares this Nigerian proverb: "A he-goat doesn't realize that he smells."[4]

That is, we cut ourselves a lot more slack than we're willing to extend to others. We either don't see that speck, don't realize that we smell, or we rationalize it all away.

Here's how I notice these tendencies in real life. When I see someone else speeding or passing in a no-passing lane, I can be quick to judge them harshly. I attribute negative motivations and qualities to them: what a jerk, how selfish. I ask, what makes *them* so important? But when *I* speed, I don't necessarily see that I am the problem. It's just that people are waiting for me. Or, I'm going fast but being careful. Or, I innocently lost track of the speed limit.

But of course, I have *no idea* why the other driver is speeding. Maybe she is being thoughtless, or maybe a loved one had an accident and she has to hurry to the hospital. Maybe when I speed, I am actually the problem and others are pointing their fingers at me! That speck in the eye? It's me.

Kendra Cherry, writing for the online publication *Verywell Mind*, explains that self-bias is a defense mechanism because it "allows you to protect your self-esteem. By attributing positive events to personal characteristics, you get a boost in confidence. By blaming outside forces for failures, you protect your self-esteem and absolve yourself from personal responsibility."[5]

Since we're wired this way, we needn't judge ourselves too harshly for falling under the spell of self-serving bias, but we can evolve. We can be mindful. We can recognize that in most conflicts, no one is either all good and blameless, or all bad and at fault. Generally, the truth lies somewhere in between.

This might be a good time to mention that I am talking here about *most* conflicts. To be clear, I am not referring to the kinds of abusive and violent "conflicts" which are really crimes. This sermon is more about the interpersonal struggles that regularly arise, and the options we have for dealing with them in a more constructive way.

One option we have, every time, is our conflict approach. There are actually five universal conflict styles to choose from. We each tend to have a dominant style, but in any given situation, we can pick any one of the five approaches.

The first conflict approach is competition—as in, this is a fight that I intend to win. Sometimes that's appropriate, though probably far less often than we might think. Still, people often fight this way, especially in relationships. The downfall of this style is that winning the battle is not the same as winning long-term happiness.

Second, is avoidance—another popular style but not always the most helpful choice. When we avoid conflict, it often ends up oozing out in very unpleasant ways. Or even exploding, like a pressure cooker. An instructor in my graduate program once told me that I was an avoider—a harsh assessment for a mediator-to-be. At the next break, I cried in the bathroom, muttering, "I do *not* avoid all conflict! I always engage in conflict with my husband." And with whom, I realized, do I have the healthiest relationship? Bingo. I suddenly saw how engaging in necessary and constructive conflict resolution is a critical element for building long-term, healthy relationships.

Third, is accommodation—really, just giving in. In many cases, this is a sensible choice, depending on the issues involved. Other times, it could be disastrous. I am frequently accommodating as a grandmother. You know, it really is fine with me to let my granddaughter pick which movie we go to rather than argue about it. On the other hand, when she and I go mountain climbing together, there is no way I'm giving in to her when her safety is at stake. Accommodating a seven-year-old in those circumstances could be tragic. Furthermore, accommodating too often could do damage to your ego; it is not healthy or happy-making to always put our own needs last.

Fourth, is compromise—which many see as the gold standard. I do not. While sometimes splitting the difference fifty-fifty works well, other times it means no one is happy. Just recently, I overheard my granddaughter and her friend arguing about whether or not to play *Apples to Apples*, which my granddaughter wanted to do. Her friend did not. The compromise they worked out was splitting the difference between how many rounds my granddaughter wanted (sixteen), and how many her friend wanted (zero). They settled on eight rounds.

I guess that solution worked. They went off to another room and I heard only cheerful sounds for the rest of their playtime. But what if they had applied the fifth conflict approach—problem solving? They might have come up with an idea that made them both happier. I think each child was conflicted by wanting what she wanted, while simultaneously wishing to be a good friend—something they could have achieved through problem solving.

Problem solving, which I consider the best conflict style to adopt, involves taking the time to figure out what each person really wants, and then trying to find a solution that incorporates each person's desires as well as possible.

That's really the trick because what the conflict is truly about is often not readily apparent. Many times, we struggle to articulate what we ourselves truly want. And if tempers are flaring, we might not even want to know what the other person is really interested in. Nothing unusual about these feelings, but if we want to problem solve, we have to listen deeply, to the other person and ourselves. We have to ask questions out of genuine curiosity in order to get to the root of the matter.

In mediator-speak, we talk about uncovering what the conflicts are about in terms of positions and interest. *Position* is what we say we want; *interest* is what needs and desires, both individual and collective, really lie at the heart of the matter.

Here's an example. A few years ago, my husband came home from the store with shampoo, as I had requested, but it was a scent I didn't like, not the vanilla he knew I wanted. I got angry, and let him know it. He, in turn, responded angrily to me. We both retreated to other rooms.

In my unhappy little corner, I had time to reflect. Wait a minute, I thought. Use your skills. What is going on here? Why are we really fighting?

I realized that I didn't feel listened to. I had told him time and time again what I liked, and still he brought me the wrong item.

So I knocked on his door, apologized for being mean, and explained my anger. I then asked what was really troubling him. He explained that he had searched for the right brand, but it wasn't there that day. He said he did know and cared about what I wanted, and had made the best choice he could. But instead of appreciation, he got yelled at. His interest was in being acknowledged for his efforts.

As for the wrong shampoo, which was my *position*, that couldn't be ignored either because the aroma of shampoo provides a daily savoring practice for me, which was actually my *interest*. Still, I realized that it was unfair to lay such a personal choice on my husband. Taking the problem solving approach, now I always buy my own shampoo!

There's a lot going on in this simple story. First, after a few minutes of miserable disconnection, working through this conflict took us one or two rungs higher on the never ending climb to building a happy, healthy relationship. We were able to bring out into the open the issues that needed to be discussed and the changes that needed to be made.

Second, understanding the true interests beneath our positions was critical to problem solving. How could we fix something when we hadn't yet identified what was actually broken?

Third, most conflicts are much more confounding. By engaging lovingly in the "great shampoo incident," Bob and I built our capacity to handle bigger, messier conflicts which are likely to emerge. Like every other skill, it takes practice.

Fourth, even though I'm an "expert," I, too, can get caught up in negative emotions and unpleasant conversations. I remain an imperfect human animal with sometimes wacky wiring! The difference is, by mindfully tapping into my conflict and happiness knowledge, I am much more likely to navigate my way back out of the holes I dig.

So, did that voice back in Stockholm that jumped into my head, saying "mediator," turn out to be welcome advice? Oh yes, quite welcome. Though I rarely work as a mediator anymore, I use conflict resolution knowledge and skills every day in some way, whether personally or professionally. Really, I think everyone should be taught how and why to engage in conflict constructively, and that education shouldn't wait until grad school! Conflict learning should be a fundamental part of everyone's daily life because it leads to better relationships and more happiness, and, helps create a better world.

Did I mention that I still don't like conflict? When conflict knocks on my door, I want to say, "Sorry, no one's home." Instead, because I know the journey to happiness includes many stops in conflict land, I try to take a deep breath and say, "Come on in." ("But don't stay too long!")

May it be so.

Forgiveness Is Beautiful

First Universalist Church and Society of Barnard
July 29, 2018

*To forgive is to set a prisoner free and discover
that the prisoner was you.*
—LEWIS B. SMEDES
*Forgive and Forget: Healing the
Hurts We Don't Deserve (1984)*

In December 2016, a remarkable event took place. US veterans who had come to help the Standing Rock Sioux block the Dakota Access Pipeline knelt before Native American elders, apologized to them, and begged for forgiveness. In a scene described in the *HuffPost*, one of the soldiers, Wesley Clark, said, in part:

> Many of us … are from the units that have hurt
> you over the many years. We came. We fought
> you. We took your land. We signed treaties that
> we broke. We stole minerals from your sacred
> hills. We blasted the faces of our presidents
> onto your sacred mountain. When we took still

more land and then we took your children ...
We didn't respect you, we polluted your Earth,
we've hurt you in so many ways but we've come
to say that we are sorry. We are at your service
and we beg for your forgiveness.[1]

And then, Lakota spiritual leader and medicine man
Chief Leonard Crow Dog forgave them. Videos of this ceremony went viral on social media, and no wonder. It was
transcendent in its beauty.

Heartfelt apologies and genuine forgiveness can be beautifully powerful in tandem, though it often doesn't work that
way. Apology and forgiveness are related, but not inseparable
(more on that later). This sermon focuses on the forgiveness
side of the reconciliation equation.

Of forgiveness, Italian psychotherapist Piero Ferrucci
describes how it "contains joy and faith in others, generosity
of spirit. Illogical and surprising, sometimes sublime, it frees
us from the ancient chains of resentment. Whoever forgives,
feels uplifted."[2]

Forgiveness is not only beautiful, it is potentially *very*
beneficial for both individual happiness and collective well-
being. Forgiveness is for *you,* the forgiver, to lay down the
burdens you've been carrying in your soul. At the same time,
by helping to stop cycles of violence and recrimination, forgiveness is peace-building, to the benefit of all.

Just thinking about forgiveness warms my heart. Yet, I
discovered early in my happiness career that not everyone
shares my warm and fuzzy feelings for forgiveness.

That realization came when I was co-facilitating an
eight-week study group on Sonja Lyubomirsky's book, *The
How of Happiness*, which includes forgiveness as one of her

science-tested strategies for increasing personal happiness. Forgiveness comes with this warning: "Of all the happiness-promoting strategies described in this book," she writes, "I believe that forgiveness is one of the most challenging to carry out."[3] Nonetheless, I recall opening the conversation that night by gushing, "I love forgiveness!" To which my dear friend Lauren, a member of the class, said, "Well I'm glad you do, Ginny, because I can't stand it."

A lively discussion ensued, letting me know people were more likely to share Lauren's perspective than my own. Yet, beautifully poignant stories of forgiveness, offered and received, nonetheless emerged that night.

No doubt, forgiveness can be emotionally thorny. Dreadful harms have been done to and by countless humans, and the pain of injury can be aroused by even talking about forgiveness. Everyone taking the time to explore this topic should be mindful of their emotions as they consider forgiveness in their own lives. I suggest focusing first on minor grievances, and saving the deepest transgressions until one feels more comfortable with the forgiveness process.

I learned that lesson during my first—and last—experience facilitating a forgiveness workshop. Rather than working with the forgiveness tools and exercises I offered, the participants wanted to rehash the pain and anger of their deepest wounds. It was all too much, too soon. As a facilitator, I was in over my head. I spent the car ride home trying to forgive myself for having served them so poorly.

By now, I get it: forgiveness can loom as a hard, unwelcome task. Still, I suspect that an antipathy toward forgiveness is often based on a misunderstanding of what forgiveness is. Probably few people think of forgiveness as a happiness strategy. It sounds almost like an oxymoron.

At the same time, even people made uneasy by for-giveness likely share my admiration for forgiveness on a heroic scale—as embodied by Nelson Mandela, for exam-ple. Together with Frederik Willem de Klerk, Mandela was awarded the Nobel Peace Prize for the peaceful dismantling of apartheid in South Africa, done largely through forgive-ness and the reconciliation process.[4]

There is also the breathtaking example of the Amish fam-ilies who, in 2006, forgave the man who killed five young girls in a one-room schoolhouse before shooting himself. At his burial, several grieving families hugged the killer's widow in a hard-to-fathom act of forgiveness.[5]

Ferrucci also writes of a friend whose father, a Jewish survivor of the Holocaust, told her the most important thing in life is "to forgive." This man lost all of his family: his first wife, his first little girl, his parents, siblings, work, and home. Yet he believed in forgiveness.

This, says Ferrucci, is what makes "civilization ... pos-sible. It is thanks to this man, and many others like him, that we have not plunged totally into barbarism."[6]

Indeed, Lyubomirsky cautions that the *lack* of forgive-ness can lead to poor behavior, from minor slights on up to outright barbarity. She says, "It appears that the natural first inclination of human beings to [various] injuries is to respond negatively, to reciprocate with equal harm."[7]

The other two typical responses she cites, avoiding the person or seeking revenge, are also troubling. However, in violent circumstances, the former is sometimes needed since avoiding an abuser to stay safe and alive can absolutely be a good choice. But for most other circumstances, Lyubomirsky writes, "It would seem obvious that such responses breed negative consequences." She explains why:

Trying to distance yourself from the transgressor—and especially trying to retaliate—ultimately makes you unhappy, damages or destroys relationships, and may even harm society at large. Throughout history and continuing through today, the drive for revenge has motivated numerous ills and horrors of our world, including murder, rape, and pillage, and also war, terrorism, and genocide.[8]

Like other happiness strategies, forgiveness matters from within our own conflicted selves right on up through international struggles. In a very real sense, the choices we make individually contribute to the greater societal zeitgeist—we are all those drops of water in the ocean. Forgiveness must be taken very seriously.

Plus, it makes us happier people.

So what is forgiveness?

Greater Good Magazine, published by The Greater Good Science Center at the University of California, Berkeley, defines forgiveness as "a conscious, deliberate decision to release feelings of resentment or vengeance toward a person or group who has harmed you, regardless of whether they actually deserve your forgiveness." This does not mean that,

> ... you deny the seriousness of an offense against you. Forgiveness does not mean forgetting, nor does it mean condoning or excusing offenses. Though forgiveness can help repair a damaged relationship, it doesn't obligate you to reconcile

with the person who harmed you, or release them from legal accountability.[9]

In other words, you forgive the *person*, not the *act*. You don't necessarily need to *ever* interact with that person again, depending on circumstances. In some cases, you may wish to work for a reconciliation that benefits all involved, which could work out beautifully. But the starting point is in your own heart and soul, and forgiving for your own well-being.

Forgiveness is also not necessarily about doing the right thing in some saintly, otherworldly way. Forgiveness can be self-centered, in a very positive way. Even in a case as extreme as forgiving the killer of the Amish schoolgirls, the Amish families themselves benefitted from their act of forgiveness. According to Amish counselor Jonas Beiler, founder of the Family Resource and Counseling Center, forgiving allowed the families to focus on their own healing.[10]

This next saying is widely but falsely attributed to the Buddha, but no matter who said it, it is still powerful: "Holding on to anger is like grasping a hot coal with the intent of throwing it at someone else; you are the one who gets burned." Forgiveness allows us to drop the coals, and heal.

It is also an act of strength. Beiler says, "Forgiveness is not for the weak. It's for people who are serious about releasing hurts. It takes a real man and a real woman to extend forgiveness and set themselves free."[11]

Television personality Oprah Winfrey puts it like this: "Forgiveness is giving up the hope that the past could have been any different ... and using this moment and this time to help yourself move forward."[12]

Dr. Fred Luskin isn't much of a celebrity, but in the forgiveness world, he's a superstar. Among other credits, he heads the Stanford University Forgiveness Projects. He says:

> The essence of forgiveness is being resilient when things don't go the way you want—to be at peace with "no," be at peace with what is, be at peace with the vulnerability inherent in human life. Then you have to move forward and live your life without prejudice.[13]

Luskin cautions, however, that "before you can forgive, you have to grieve." Then, it is a choice. Luskin says we can choose whether to dwell on past hurts or try to see the good in others. "The same free will that allows everybody to screw up allows us all to choose all the incredible goodness we do."[14]

When and how to make that choice is up to you. Way back in that study group, I mentioned that I was nursing some hard feelings toward my granddaughter's father. One of the participants demanded to know why I hadn't forgiven him yet. Because I wasn't ready; not enough time had passed. Ultimately, I forgave him—but don't let anybody tell you when to do your forgiving. Process the pain. Grieve. Rage if need be. It's your timetable.

I hope you eventually get there. It's worth the effort. According to Lyubomirsky: "Forgiving people are less likely to be hateful, depressed, hostile, anxious, angry, and neurotic. They are more likely to be happier, healthier, more agreeable, and more serene."[15]

Given that healthy relationships are the number one ingredient of happiness, this just makes sense. I have at least three very close friends who make me happy, but who once made me so angry that I wanted to throw each of those friendships out the window. Forever. It took time with each relationship, but eventually I was able to fully forgive each friend—and myself—and fully embrace the friendship. I am so grateful for forgiveness.

To be clear, there are others whom I've forgiven while also making the choice that I no longer wanted those relationships in my life. Forgiveness and repairing relationships, like forgiveness and apology, are close partners, but not inseparable.

And, Lord only knows how many people have chosen to forgive me, especially my children and husband, for which I am also deeply grateful.

Poet and author David Whyte frames this beautifully: "All friendships of any length are based on a continued, mutual forgiveness. Without tolerance and mercy all friendships die."[16]

Here's more from the Greater Good Science Center. They relay that forgiveness is good for our mental health, and may help prevent suicide; it is good for our physical health, especially our immune systems; and it boosts kindness and connectedness—both indispensable to a happier life.[17]

But how does one go about practicing forgiveness?

First, proceed with caution. It can be complicated and nuanced. Try not to expose yourself to additional harm. Remember that it is a process, it can be messy, and each person's path will be unique. That said, here are some tips.

Luskin, who is also the author of *Forgive for Good*, offers his research-tested "Nine Steps to Forgiveness." These steps include being able to articulate what happened that is not okay, making "a commitment to yourself to feel better," and knowing you don't necessarily have to reconcile "with the person who upset you or [condone] the action." He also suggests "stress management to soothe your body's fight or flight response." And to "give up expecting things from your life or from other people that they do not choose to give you."[18]

Mindfulness, the foundation for so many happiness strategies, is key here, too. In her book, *Triumph of the Heart: Forgiveness in an Unforgiving World*, journalist Megan Feldman Bettencourt says you can "nurture the 'forgiveness instinct' by becoming more self-aware of your role in conflicts." She also encourages mindfulness meditation, "because it enhances the parts of the brain researchers affiliate with empathy, problem-solving, and positive mood."[19] All are crucial qualities to use in the forgiveness process.

With mindfulness, we can better appreciate our own role in creating painful situations and also practice self-forgiveness on our way to forgiving others. Because, in reality, none of us are saints. Martin Luther King, Jr. said, "We must develop and maintain the capacity to forgive.... There is some good in the worst of us and some evil in the best of us. When we discover this, we are less prone to hate our enemies."[20]

In my own domestic sphere, a much smaller scale than the one to which Reverend King may have been referring, I have found that remembering the good in someone who has hurt me, or even just irked me, is so helpful in moving toward forgiveness. Seeing the whole person, and a fuller history of our relationship (including my own missteps), puts the harm into a much more manageable perspective.

Here's another strategy you could try: writing letters. The letter could be offering forgiveness or seeking forgiveness. Writing is a very powerful exercise, but it is important to keep in mind that you do not need to actually *deliver* the letter, especially if your situation is not emotionally or physically safe. At any point in the forgiveness process, safety should always be paramount. In some circumstances, you may wish to have actual contact with the person who harmed you. If you were the transgressor, it is possible that the person you harmed may not want any contact from you. It is also possible that you *could* deliver the letter, and that letter could lead to a profound shift in your relationship with the letter's reader. However it plays out in your situation, the very act of writing a forgiveness letter and naming what needs to be named can help *you* move forward through the forgiveness process.

Shortly after that first study group session, I decided to meditate on forgiveness, which is an ongoing practice. Much to my surprise, it was like opening Ma and Pa Kettle's closet. On that old-timey radio show, there was a funny closet routine where Ma regularly told Pa not to open the closet. Of course, he did anyway, and out tumbled all kinds of belongings crammed into that space.

That's how it was when I opened the closet during my forgiveness meditation. So many "unforgivens" tumbled out. Whoa! So many hot coals I'd been carrying around without even realizing it.

Unlike Ma Kettle, though, I'm going to suggest you do open those closets. Carefully—no need to get reinjured. But just think what you can clean out! Imagine all the unforgivens, the burning coals impeding your happiness, and you don't even remember them! It could be a spring cleaning like no other.

Finally, I want to return to self-forgiveness which is probably the most valuable place to start being a more forgiving person. I often think, if a friend said to us the kinds of things we say to ourselves, that person wouldn't be a friend anymore. Forgiving ourselves allows us to be more at peace, to thrive, to be resilient and hopeful, and to move on. It's a practice that builds greater skill and faith in forgiving others.

To be clear, forgiving ourselves, like when forgiving others, doesn't necessarily mean condoning any harmful actions we may have taken. I see it as a moral responsibility to take steps to repair damage, when we can.

This brings me back to apology. So often, when someone has been hurt, they just want an apology! A sincere apology, that takes into account what the harm might have felt like from the other person's perspective, may encourage the other person to forgive us. However, apologies and forgiveness are not transactional. We may want, but never receive, an apology from those who have injured us, sometimes grievously. With or without the apology, we still have the power to forgive.

Similarly, when I offer an apology, there can be no strings attached: i.e., "I will sincerely apologize to you but only if you forgive me." Rather, I must simply mean: "*I. Am. Sorry.*" And possibly, "What can I do to make it better?" The other person doesn't even have to accept my apology. This is the risk I take in offering up what to me is the moral choice—a risk that comes with no guarantees.

It doesn't always feel good to acknowledge having hurt another, but it happens. We all slip up, accidentally and on purpose. This is another area where I find Ben-Shahar's "permission to be human" wisdom helpful. Remembering that I am human helps me curb my hubris, and to be more forgiving of my failures. One researcher found that Iceland is an especially happy country because people there are allowed to fail. To be human. To accept that making mistakes is part of moving forward.

Forgiving failure is for more than just our own hearts. Our planet needs us to get over ourselves and try again in order to address all of the significant challenges we face. What if that approach to climate action didn't work? Try again. Or what if that approach to parenting didn't work? Try again. Failure plus forgiveness paves the way for progress.

For ourselves, for others, forgiveness is the beautiful gift which allows us all to bloom more fully.

We can all do this. As Piero Ferrucci says, "If we find in ourselves the place where we feel happy and whole, forgiveness is already a fact. Forgiveness becomes the easiest thing in the world: It is not something we do, but something we *are*.... We have only to give ourselves permission to be so."[21]

We have only to give ourselves permission.

Forgiveness can be something we are.

And we can be beautiful.

May it be so.

The Interconnected Happiness of Humans and Other Animals

First Universalist Church and Society of Barnard
August 5, 2018

It is through this mysterious power that we too have our being, and we therefore yield to our neighbors, even to our animal neighbors, the same right as ourselves to inhabit this vast land.

—SITTING BULL

On a lovely summer day, as I was driving to my friend Betsy's house for a work project, I heard an NPR segment about the president's plan to substantially revise the Endangered Species Act. While this act has successfully protected vulnerable plants and animals from extinction for over forty years, NPR noted that the "landmark law has also grown politically divisive. Republicans and industry groups say it hurts economic growth."[1] In the story, Greg Sheehan from the US Fish and Wildlife Service said the administration wants to make sure we don't have "overreaching provisions on our society and our local communities and our private landowners in America."

Economic growth versus species extinction? Rights of private landowners versus species extinction? I was disgusted.

Fortunately, Betsy had a bat trapped in her sunroom. I say fortunately, because as she was trying to gently guide the bat outdoors, she said to me, "Just another of God's creatures trying to make its way through the world."

Her words were a balm to my spirit. Together, the two points of view bookend our cultural views on animals today. Except for beloved pets, our GDP-driven society all too often sees animals largely through the lens of profit or loss. How else to explain putting economic growth and private property above the right to exist at all? Betsy's offhand remark came from the other end of the spectrum: the idea that all life is worthy, and deserving of happiness, or at least well-being.

Further, the happiness and well-being of humans and other animals is deeply connected. For clarity, I am using the word "animals" to mean all members of Kingdom Animalia, which includes insects, arachnids, reptiles, fish, crustaceans, birds, and mammals. Our very survival as a species, and the survival of many animal species as well, is interdependent. We need each other.

This interdependence was poignantly illustrated at a house concert I attended featuring Newfoundland musician Rik Barron. Barron told a story about the demise of the cod fishing industry which decimated lives and villages up and down the North Atlantic Coast. His haunting ballad about a former fisherman shooting a rifle into his now useless boat provided the perfect example of the connection between animal well-being and human happiness—or lack thereof.

Barron's ballad intrigued me, so I went online to learn more. I read that in 1992, Canada declared a moratorium on the Northern Cod fishery which had been thriving for almost five centuries. According to the Newfoundland and Labrador Heritage website, "The moratorium put about 30,000 people in the province out of work and ended a way of life that had endured for generations in many outport communities."[2] Five hundred years, and then it ended, thanks to massive overfishing.

That overfishing, in turn, was due to technological progress, ecological ignorance, governmental mismanagement, and socioeconomic factors like cultural identity, livelihood, and investment in equipment and infrastructure. It was complicated, but "when the government failed to intervene—due largely to the highly sensitive nature of the political discourse—the ecosystem was brought past its threshold and collapsed, leaving everyone worse off."[3]

Everyone. Especially the cod, which almost went extinct. Happily, that fish is slowly rebounding, but worldwide, the tragedy of human interests overpowering the survival capacity of other species continues to play out, often in ways that make humans unhappy also.

Take for example the massive red tide covering hundreds of miles of the Southwest Florida coast for many months in 2018, starting in the summer and continuing through late fall. The Weather Channel reported that the red tide left "droves of dead animals, including an 'unprecedented' number of sea turtles…. Pelicans, double-crested cormorants and mallard and mottled ducks" were also affected. The death toll even included dolphins and manatees. And experts say, "the wildlife found dead on the beaches or on the surface of the ocean is only a fraction of the actual toll…. Most of the dead animals sink to the bottom of the ocean."[4] Florida's governor, Rick Scott, declared the red tide situation an emergency.[5]

During the red tide, humans were also vulnerable to respiratory ailments and vomiting. Plus, it was seriously unpleasant. One fishing guide quoted by the Weather Channel said, "It smells like massive death."

The Weather Channel explained that red tides are a natural occurrence, but when they "move closer to shore, they are capable of using man-made nutrients from runoff for their growth." While human activity may not have incited the 2018 red tide, it's likely that fertilizer used for farming crops such as tomatoes and sugarcane—which creates the nutrient-rich runoff upon which the algae can feed—significantly exacerbated the problem, condemning numerous innocent species to death.

Many residents and passionate animal lovers were deeply distressed by the carnage. The red tide also created many unhappy beachgoers, negatively impacting the tourism industry. It's not yet clear how devastating the red tides will be in years to come, but according to the Environmental Protection Agency, "as air and ocean temperatures increase, the environment becomes more hospitable to toxic algal blooms in several ways," and thus, the prospects are gloomy for both sea animals and the humans who love them. Researchers warn that "climate change will severely affect our ability to control blooms, and in some cases could make it near impossible."[6]

Climate change is also posing a severe threat to animals in my own landlocked state of Vermont. Vermont Public Radio's *Outdoor Radio* series has reported on the fatal threat that global warming poses to our iconic moose. The threat comes in the form of ticks, many, many thousands of them—enough to collectively kill the large, beloved mammals.[7] It is not just the moose that is in danger. VPR also reports that forest fragmentation, which "occurs when large tracts of woods are bought up, parceled out, and cleared ... may be the leading cause behind the decline of Vermont forest-bird species such as the Canada Warbler and the Winter Wren."[8]

So, fewer moose and fewer songbirds in Vermont (the Green Mountain State) thanks to climate change and forest fragmentation—both by-products of human activity. Our species is definitely wreaking havoc on well-being across the animal world. The impacts are devastating for the species under threat, but quite selfishly, the losses are also devastating for us. Imagine what it would be like if we lost all our moose and all our songbirds! At the least, the daily quality of our human lives would be heartbreakingly diminished. Our happiness is connected.

Now might be a good time to fess up: I'm actually not an animal lover. Oh, I get excited about spotting a moose or a bear, and certainly appreciate a good bird song, but I've always been much more interested in humans. We're one of the rare Vermont households without a dog. We do have a cat, but only because I saw a chipmunk scurry across the kitchen floor one day and knew I had to do something. Though we are affectionate with our kitty, Applesauce, she receives much more enthusiastic loving from the upstairs tenants.

I make this point to emphasize that I do not approach the issue of animal well-being with a bleeding heart for all things great and small. I am rather late in recognizing that animals are sentient beings and just as deserving of a place on the planet as humans are.

Understanding the depth of environmental degradation and the urgency of climate change has brought me well along the road of esteeming other species. I've traveled so far that, even though I'm not a theologian, I'm going to go out on a biblical limb. That is, I can't help but wonder if the Christian "human dominion" belief system, often interpreted as supe-riority and control over the natural world, isn't seriously problematic. I believe this attitude has disconnected us from nature and warped our hearts and laws.

Why, for example, do so many people condone trophy hunting? Killing beautiful living animals, vital members of their ecosystems, just for a rug or a decoration on a wall, and for boasting rights? I heard one trophy hunter on a radio show say he kills these animals simply "because I can." How can this be good for our souls? No doubt, money plays a role. I'm sure it is profitable for gaming outfits to facilitate this senseless killing.

We are asking the same questions about factory farm-ing and the many reports of animal abuse occurring in order to obtain more efficient, profitable food production. People need affordable food, of course, but I think we can do better. I mean, how in our heart of hearts can we participate in such horrid animal suffering for *any* human purpose? Jonathan Safran Foer, author of *Eating Animals*, observes:

> Perhaps in the back of our minds we already understand, without all the science I've discussed, that something terribly wrong is happening. Our sustenance now comes from misery. We know that if someone offers to show us a film on how our meat is produced, it will be a horror film. We perhaps know more than we care to admit, keep-ing it down in the dark places of our memory—disavowed. When we eat factory-farmed meat we

live, literally, on tortured flesh. Increasingly, that
tortured flesh is becoming our own.[9]

For our own spiritual growth, peace of mind, and healthy
bodies, we need public policies that honor the innate value
of all sentient beings. That is something our current Gross
Domestic Product system just does not do. It is, however, a
goal my good friend and Gross National Happiness USA colleague Beth Allgood is working toward. In 2017, she came to
Montpelier, Vermont, to share her expertise in a presentation
entitled, "True Well-Being for Animals and People," based on
an International Fund for Animal Welfare (IFAW) report she
co-authored. The report was released at the Convention of
Biological Diversity in 2017.

Jane Goodall, the world-renowned anthropologist best
known for her work on behalf of chimpanzees, wrote the
introduction to the IFAW report. She said in part: "The
health of our communities is interwoven with the health of
our natural landscapes, and the decisions we make affect
every animal, including humans, on this planet. We must find
a new measurement of personal and societal success, one that
is environmentally sustainable, and culturally and economi-
cally inclusive."[10]

At the Montpelier presentation, Allgood highlighted the
many ways animals add to human well-being. For starters,
taking care of animals can build empathy in children. Animals
also ease loneliness, which is epidemic today. Bees pollinate
our fruits and nuts, highly valuable sources of human well-
being. Bats eat mosquitoes, including those carrying West Nile
Virus which is potentially fatal for humans. And then there is
the opossum, which can eat thousands of deer ticks every year.
Chickens eat ticks, too—lots of ticks! Allgood believes:

Measuring success solely through the lens of GDP
ultimately does not support animals or people....
People benefit when we conserve and protect wildlife and treat companion and agricultural animals
humanely. Understanding this, we can now bring
animal welfare and conservation into social, environmental, and economic policies.[11]

Worldwide, the need is urgent. A report issued by a team
of US and Canadian researchers, led by Cornell University
Laboratory of Ornithology's Ken Rosenberg, found that
there are almost three billion fewer songbirds in North
America as of 2019 than there were in 1970, "nearly 30% of
the total [population], and even common birds such as spar-
rows and blackbirds are in decline...."[12] In Africa, according
to Allgood, more than one elephant is killed by ivory poach-
ers every thirty minutes—alarmingly, a number that is higher
than the elephants' birth rates. Allgood says, our system has
made "ivory worth more than elephants." Protected by the
Endangered Species Act, the North Atlantic right whale is
also in grave danger. Many are being killed by ship strikes.
Large freighters all too often run over whales swimming on
the surface of the sea, with the giant propellers fatally injur-
ing the animal. NOAA Fisheries reports, "researchers esti-
mate there are about 400 North Atlantic right whales in the
population with fewer than 100 breeding females left."[13]

The details are different, from cod to sea turtles to moose,
elephants, and whales, but the bottom line is the same. The
world's animals are in jeopardy. Scientists have declared that
we are in the sixth mass extinction, the first mass extinction
resulting primarily from human activity. This is a systemic

problem that calls for a dramatic change in our economic and political structures. Allgood says, "When I first heard of Gross National Happiness it hit me like lightning ... the extinction crisis adds urgency to broaden ways we measure now, before these wild animals and habitats are gone."

Allgood did share *some* good news at her Montpelier presentation: An IFAW poll in the United States found that 90 percent of respondents believe that being around pets contributes to an individual's happiness, and 85 percent said that the ability to view wildlife in their native habitat is happy-making as well.[14] Ninety and 85 percent—that's a remarkable consensus in the US today!

Those numbers are heartening because it's a definite challenge to convince people that moving from Gross Domestic Product to Gross National Happiness is a) possible and b) a promising path forward for a sustainable future. If all the animal lovers out there begin to understand that GNH may offer the best hope of saving species from extinction, that could be a huge boost to the still very young GNH movement.

Maybe that's just another way of using animals for human purposes. I don't think so, though. I really do care about most animals, so much so that I'm urging my GNHUSA colleagues to add another domain to the well-being policy framework modeled after that originally developed in Bhutan. That domain would be *animal well-being*—just as deserving of policy consideration as any of the other elements that support human happiness.

Truthfully, no one needs to choose animals over humans, or humans over animals. *New York Times* columnist Nicholas Kristof, whose compassion and insight always inspire me, writes,

> I wonder: Does honoring animal rights come at the expense of human rights? ... Are we betraying our own species when we write checks to help gorillas (or puppies or wild horses)? Is it wrongheaded to fight for elephants and rhinos (or farm animals at home) while five million children still die each year before the age of five?

He concludes, "I've come to believe that on the contrary, conserving rhinos or gorillas—or speaking up for tortured farm animals at home—is good for humans, too."[15]

Kristof cites the example of the Dzanga Sangha Protected Areas, which "hires 240 local people, from rangers to trackers who locate the gorillas and get them habituated to people." Without this project, Kristof writes, it could be the end of the forest and the end of the BaAka pygmies' culture and identity.

Hmmm ... the end of the forest, and therefore an end to the humans' culture and identity? Sounds a lot like the North Atlantic coast—with the collapse of the cod population, the fishermen lost their livelihoods, identities, and culture.

Of course, there are many factors contributing to all these situations. It's not all about greed, or landowner rights, or a growth economy. Indeed, the GNH approach recognizes the importance of a vital economy, along with a wide range of other well-being factors. One of Allgood's case studies focused on an impoverished village in Malawi, where a river was the only water and protein source. At the river, crocodiles and hippos killed villagers. Elephants presented another threat: they raided the villagers' crops.

In this situation, IFAW helped villagers create a GNH approach—that is, a holistic solution respecting the varied needs of all involved, human and animal. The solution included a fence to keep the elephants out, along with a well, fishponds, and water to irrigate local gardens. These interventions meant the girls didn't have to fetch water from the river that was miles away; instead, they could go to school. Building water fences kept the people safe while respecting the well-being of the crocodiles and the hippos.

This example shows how a GNH policy approach can work to the advantage of both humans and other animals. The real barrier is not an inability to craft policy; it is getting to the point where it matters enough to invest the effort. A place, in other words, where elephants' lives are worth more than their tusks. And cheap meat is not worth the expense of massive animal suffering.

I don't know how we get there without a massive spiritual shift away from human dominion and toward a deeply internalized, collective appreciation of all sentient beings: bats trapped in the sunroom, songbirds in fragmented forests, sea turtles in the red tide, and even hungry crocodiles. Yes, because even their existence is worthwhile.

Until we realize that transformation, let's at least recognize that our own selfish interests are causing harm, and demand that we take better care of the rest of the animal kingdom.

As Allgood and her co-authors on the IFAW report stress, "The fate of mankind is so closely intertwined with biodiversity and a healthy planet that we cannot exist without it. The entire web of life is interconnected and we should be motivated to protect animals because our actions are the greatest threat to their survival and their extinction is the greatest threat to ours."[16]

Albert Einstein says we must widen "our circle of compassion, to embrace all living beings and all of nature."[17] Indeed, we must, but compassion is not enough. We also need to act, and quickly—enacting new laws and regulations based on a change of heart that soundly rejects the exploitative concept of human dominion over animals. That rejection also means stepping away from the GDP's money-driven approach that values animals primarily for their dollar worth to humans. When we use, instead, an alternative measures framework, like GNH, that values and considers a wide range of well-being factors, including our interdependent relationship with animals, then we can channel the compassion to much more effectively build a happier world for *all* the species who live here.

May it be so.

Kindness: Our Best Tool for Personal and Collective Wholeness

First Universalist Church and Society of Barnard
August 12, 2018

*Nothing can make our life, or the lives of other
people, more beautiful than perpetual kindness.*
—LEO TOLSTOY
*A Calendar of Wisdom: Daily Thoughts to
Nourish the Soul, Written and Selected
from the World's Sacred Texts (1997)*

You might have noticed that an ongoing exploration of personal and collective happiness can cover some pretty rough territory. It's not always fun. Genuine happiness—which can be described as wholeness, growing into our most thriving selves—must be built on reality, not on the shifting sands of denial or suppression. If we want to be whole, if we want to contribute to a more whole world, we must honestly face what needs to be done, systemically and individually, in order to cultivate happiness and well-being for all.

Fortunately, we have kindness to help us. In Piero Ferrucci's book on this subject, he acknowledges that it may seem absurd to consider kindness in a world so "full of violence, war, terrorism [and] devastation. And yet," he observes, "life goes on precisely because we are kind to one another."[1]

The Dalai Lama, in his preface to Ferrucci's book, wrote, "If we stop to think, it is clear that our very survival ... depends upon the acts and kindness of so many people.... On the other hand, the more our hearts and minds are afflicted with ill will, the more miserable we become. Therefore, we cannot avoid the necessity of kindness and compassion."

I agree. Of course, who am I to disagree with the Dalai Lama? Still, it seems worth emphasizing: kindness is not only one of the loveliest tools in our happiness toolkits—kits we all have as a birth right—but also a necessary one.

I keep a sign in my bedroom window, and I see the same sign posted in many other homes and businesses. It says: "In this house, we believe: black lives matter, women's rights are human rights, no human is illegal, science is real, love is love, kindness is everything."

Kindness *is* everything. This phrase is also the name of the organization founded by Jennifer Rosen-Heinz that began making this sign available to all those households, including mine. (The idea came from a handmade sign created by a woman in Madison, Wisconsin.) Proceeds then went to the ACLU—a good example of how kindness begets kindness.[2]

I used to puzzle over what the saying "kindness is everything" truly means. But I have come to see—as both the Dalai Lama and Ferrucci point out—that without kindness, it is doubtful that humanity could even survive, much less move toward healing and wholeness. Every day the news brings stories of humans behaving in ways utterly devoid of kindness—wrenching, horrifying behaviors. The bleakness of a world where kindness is completely absent is beyond imagining.

Clearly, on every level—self, community, nation, and the planet—we all need more kindness. Happily, according to psychologist Dacher Keltner, author of *Born to Be Good: The Science of a Meaningful Life*, "our mammalian and hominid evolution have crafted a species—us—with remarkable tendencies toward kindness."[3] Thus, kindness need not be a scarce resource. Theoretically, kindness can flow abundantly.

One way to let kindness flow freely is by paying careful attention to what it is that we are paying attention to. The world is too vast and complex for us to observe more than a fraction of it at a time. "There's a great big, beautiful world out there that a lot of normal folks are just barely taking in," says Temple Grandin, a renowned expert on both autism and animal behavior.[4] She captures so beautifully the phenomenon of our capacity to either see or not see so much of what is right in front of our noses. Too often what we see depends on what we're looking for.

This applies to kindness as well. If we keep our antennae raised for annoying behaviors, or worse, we'll see them. I would never suggest ignoring real concerns, but at the same time, we can consciously choose to be on alert for kindness. Sometimes it's hard to see because kindness can be so normal, it's almost invisible. Other times, it's a bit out of the ordinary, and therefore more visible. On occasion, kindness is truly extraordinary, like when a nurse I know gave a month of her life to care for Syrian refugees who survived the perilous ocean journey to Greece.

We all know how to be kind, in ways large and small. Even smiles and waves can be meaningful acts of kindness. There's a value to taking the time to soak in the many kindnesses around us each day. One of Tal Ben-Shahar's pithy sayings is, "What we appreciate, appreciates."[5] That is, what we take the time to value grows in importance in our lives and likely, therefore, grows in quantity as well. Appreciating good deeds helps us to savor the kindness of others and reminds us to be kinder people, ourselves.

We need those reminders. In our hectic lives, we often know the right thing to do, but we don't always take action. Buddhist meditation teacher Katy Brennan says kindness needs to be a moral discipline. "Although human kindness is deeply natural and instinctive," she writes, "it can also be shaky and unstable. In our present mode of existence, self-ishness and mindlessness compete and often trump kindness and mindfulness."[6]

I know what she's talking about. I carry with me a piece of turtle shell from a turtle I could have been kind to, but wasn't. It was trying to cross a quiet country road. When I saw it, I thought the turtle might not make it, that I should maybe carry it to the other side. But ... I kept driving. Selfish? Mindless? I don't know. The next day, I came upon the flat-tened turtle. Pieces of shell were strewn over the pavement. Of course, I felt terrible. If I had heeded my kindness instinct, that turtle presumably would not have died. I picked up a piece of its shell and keep it as a reminder: When the oppor-tunity arises to be kind, seize that opportunity.

This reminder is not just for the real or metaphorical turtles we come upon—giving kindness is good for us, too. Ferrucci's uncle is the English writer Aldous Huxley, who studied many ways to develop "human potential, including such diverse approaches as Vedanta, psychedelics, bodywork, meditation, hypnotic trance, and Zen." In the end, according to Ferrucci, Huxley said, "People often ask me what is the most effective technique for transforming their life. It is a little embarrassing that after years and years of research and experimentation, I have to say that the best answer is—just be a little kinder."[7]

Just be a little kinder. So simple—when we pay attention.

The science of happiness has also chimed in with this sweet news: "Kindness Makes You Happy ... and Happiness Makes You Kind." According to Alex Dixon, writing in *Greater Good Magazine,* "new research suggests that once you start doing nice things for other people, you might not want to stop." He says, it's almost as if "you could walk into a store and buy lifelong happiness" because your "kindness might create a virtuous cycle that promotes lasting happiness and altruism."[8]

That's not all kindness does for us. Lyubomirsky's book *The How of Happiness* lists multiple ways that the practice of kindness can make us feel better: we perceive others more positively, we nurture cooperative communities, we feel thankful for good fortune, and our improved self-perception as good people leads to "greater confidence, optimism, and usefulness." Also, kindness "promotes a sense of meaningfulness and value" in life and can create "a cascade of positive social consequences."[9]

Organizational consultant Birju Pandya, who focuses on systems evolution and personal transformation, lists "5 Ways Science Says Kindness Will Change Your Life":

1. Kindness rewires our minds for greater health.
2. Small shifts can grow our capacity for kindness.

3. Kindness can help the bottom line [because] the single greatest advantage in the modern economy is a happy and engaged workforce.

4. Your social community benefits from small acts of kindness.

5. Change yourself with kindness, change the world with kindness.

He explains, "As we are increasingly in a world where most are unhappy in their day-to-day life, kindness offers an alternative for both personal benefit and potentially greater social benefit."[10]

Of course I love the concept of changing ourselves, and then the world, with kindness. That's the core of this book—personal and collective transformation. And what better place to start than with kindness?

But there's more to kindness than we might realize. Irish writer John O'Donohue sees its beautiful side:

> The word kindness has a gentle sound that seems to echo the presence of compassionate goodness. When someone is kind to you, you feel understood and seen. There is no judgment or harsh perception directed toward you. Kindness has gracious eyes; it is not small-minded or competitive; it wants nothing back for itself. Kindness strikes a resonance with the depths of your own heart; it also suggests that your vulnerability, though somehow exposed, is not taken advantage of; rather, it has become an occasion for dignity and empathy. Kindness casts a different light,

an evening light that has the depth of color and patience to illuminate what is complex and rich in difference.[11]

A more utilitarian perspective comes from psychoanalyst Adam Phillips and historian Barbara Taylor in their 2009 book, *On Kindness*. They say kindness can be "sympathy, generosity, altruism, benevolence, humanity, compassion, pity, empathy ... they all denote what the Victorians called 'open-heartedness,' the sympathetic expansiveness linking self to other."[12]

Here's a third view of kindness from *Psychology Today* blogger Karyn Hall:

> Kindness is defined as the quality of being friendly, generous, and considerate. Affection, gentleness, warmth, concern, and care are words that are associated with kindness. While kindness has a connotation of meaning someone is naïve or weak, that is not the case. Being kind often requires courage and strength. Kindness is an interpersonal skill.[13]

Wait a minute—Hall says kindness is seen, albeit falsely, as naïve or weak? Or as Phillips and Taylor put it, "Most people, as they grow up now, secretly believe that kindness is a virtue of losers."[14] What? How can this be so?

I first learned of Phillips and Taylor through Maria Popova, the curator of the magnificent *Brain Pickings* website. In an essay titled, "How Kindness Became Our Forbidden Pleasure," Popova observes how:

At some point in recent history, kindness became little more than an abstract aspiration, its concrete practical applications a hazardous and vulnerable-making behavior to be avoided—we need only look to the internet's "outrage culture" for evidence, or to the rise of cynicism as our flawed self-defense mechanism against the perceived perils of kindness. We've come to see the emotional porousness that kindness requires as a dangerous crack in the armor of the independent self, an exploitable outward vulnerability—too high a cost to pay for the warm inward balm of the benevolence for which we long in the deepest parts of ourselves.[15]

Despite Popova's warning, I read the Phillips and Taylor book with eager anticipation on summer vacation. It did not make me happy. Rather, their history was deeply upsetting, detailing politicians and philosophers through the ages who found kindness too subversive for their winner-take-all and dog-eat-dog economic and governing structures. Over time, kindness became marginalized as a quality for women, especially mothers, and a few outlier professions like ministers.

Intellectually, I believe Popova, and Phillips and Taylor. However, their conclusion is completely unacceptable to me. If kindness is a forbidden pleasure, and somehow subversive, I say, let us boldly rebel, reclaim kindness as a human right, and spread it about openly and even flamboyantly!

I have to admit, the culture of the United States these days does seem to be substantially less kind—an observation backed up by a November 2019 article in *The Atlantic,* titled, "America's Epidemic of Unkindness." The title is pretty bleak, but the subtitle sounds like we'll have company in unleashing an uprising of kindness: "A new research institute at UCLA wants to start a virtuous cycle of generosity and do-gooding."

That new institute, according to author Annie Lowrey, is the Bedari Kindness Institute at UCLA. Lowrey says, "There is a sweeping scientific case for kindness. In some ways, modern life has made us unkind. That unkindness has profound personal effects. And if we can build a kinder society, that would make life better for everyone."[16]

Despite the epidemic of unkindness that Lowrey reports, I personally experience kindness frequently. Maybe that's just Vermont. And maybe the fact that I am a middle-class white woman also has something to do with that.

Ta-Nehisi Coates, a contemporary American journalist and writer from Baltimore, Maryland, opened my eyes to the privilege aspect of kindness. In his book, *Between the World and Me,* he writes of moving to Paris, where a new friend was kind to him. Nonetheless, Coates remained guarded:

> Was this all some elaborate ritual to get an angle on me? My friend paid. I thanked him. But when we left, I made sure he walked out first. He wanted to show me one of those old buildings that seem to be around every corner in that city. And the entire time he was leading me, I was sure he was going to make a quick turn into an alley, where some dudes would be waiting to strip me of what, exactly? But my new friend simply showed me the building, shook my hand, gave a fine bonne soirée, and walked off into the wide open night.

And watching him walk away, I felt that I had missed part of the experience because my eyes were made in Baltimore, because my eyes were blindfolded by fear.[17]

Coates' story is dreadfully sad. Before I read this passage, I never realized that both giving and receiving kindness involve a certain degree of vulnerability. Kindness is not always available or safe for everyone. When even the capacity to give and receive kindness can be limited by skin color, well, that's tragic. It's yet another reason to work toward dismantling white supremacy.

In the meantime, those of us who are less vulnerable such that we can practice kindness more freely might be more generous with our kindnesses, and even more grateful for the opportunities we have to be kind.

And we can all exercise greater care. For starters, we can consider that *a lack of kindness*—not sending a card, not inquiring after a family member's health—might be inadvertently hurtful. Not that we can always be there for everyone, but it's something to be aware of.

Indeed, kindness takes discernment. Is this the right thing to do, at the right time? Even though giving makes us feel good, kindness is really about the other person. Certainly, we don't want to be patronizing. Giving someone something they don't want or need might feel good to the giver, but it isn't actually kind. For example, after natural disasters, we might think sending our gently-used clothing to survivors is helpful, only to burden them with piles of used clothes when what they desperately need is money, or a place to live (in which to put the clothes). It's good to consider, is your gift wanted and needed? Would another choice be better?

Chapter Ten

In addition to being thoughtful about the kindness we extend to others, we also need to be kind to ourselves. We can't keep saying "yes" when we are depleted or when the kindness needed is just too hard. Still, sometimes we have to give anyway. I don't particularly enjoy cooking, yet when there's a neighborhood meal train set up for a community member in need, I do my duty and sign up. It's part of nurturing a healthy community. Sometimes a grieving friend needs extra attention when I might rather be hiking; in those times, the hike can wait. It can be hard to be there for people who are suffering. Kindness can take courage, perseverance, even a strong stomach. And of course, kindness requires mindfulness, including awareness that you do not deplete your own resources.

Here is a kindness truism I don't believe: "Tis better to give than to receive." Actually, both are necessary. If we're all intent on giving, who will receive our kindness? A couple winters ago, a passing stranger saw me struggling to get my car out of an icy driveway and he stopped to help. After my car was unstuck, and I'd thanked him, he replied, "No, thank *you* for giving me the chance to do something nice today." My receiving was actually also giving to him.

Another kindness cliché I don't believe is that it is better to be anonymous in your giving. There may be occasions when that is the right choice, but anonymity means the recipient doesn't know who to thank. It may feel like the high road, when really, we're depriving someone else of the opportunity to express gratitude.

Once while walking, I found five, one-hundred-dollar bills in the grass next to the road, along with several pieces of mail that presumably identified the owner. This was just down the street from a middle school, so I went there and learned that, yes, the name on the mail was one of their parents. When I handed over the money, the secretary asked for my name. I declined, saying my identity wasn't important.

But maybe it was. I didn't need to be thanked, but maybe *they* needed to thank me.

That story illustrates another point. There can be a lot going on with any single act of kindness—so many decisions, choices, and layers. Ferrucci's kindness book lists eighteen different qualities which he says are necessary to cultivate true kindness: honesty, warmth, forgiveness, contact, sense of belonging, trust, mindfulness, empathy, humility, patience, generosity, respect, flexibility, memory, loyalty, gratitude, service, and joy.

Paradoxically, though, kindness can also be quite simple. In the words of Nkosi Johnson, a South African boy who died from HIV when he was twelve years old, "Do all you can, with what you have, in the time you have, in the place where you are."[18]

The Dalai Lama says, kindness is his religion, so it seems fitting to give him the final word: "Be kind whenever possible. It is always possible."[19]

May it be so.

Attitude of Gratitude

First Universalist Church and Society of Barnard
August 19, 2018

*As we express our gratitude, we must never
forget that the highest appreciation is not to
utter words, but to live by them.*
— JOHN F. KENNEDY
"Thanksgiving Proclamation" (1963)

I like to believe you've all had moments in life when you felt a tender, unexpected rush of gratitude. Maybe the feeling sprang from a momentous development, like receiving a good medical diagnosis or a hard-earned diploma. Or, the gratitude was sparked more gently, perhaps by spying the first flowers of spring. With gratitude, size doesn't matter. What matters is the glow in your heart.

Almost every Sunday evening I feel this glow, especially on chillier nights when there's a literal glow from the wood stove in the kitchen. Our Sunday suppers are simple but treasured affairs: homemade soup with bread (often, an olive loaf) and garlic oil with cloves from our garden. We light candles, turn on the colored lights, and pour some wine—

white for my husband, red for me. This is our time to marvel at the abundance of our lives.

Maybe you have a treasured ritual or a stockpile of deeply satisfying gratitude experiences stored in your heart which brought you joy in the moment and continue to do so in the remembering. But what makes gratitude even sweeter is that it does so much more than provide pleasure in the moment. Over the long haul, gratitude is good for our own well-being and also may benefit the broader community.

In fact, gratitude is so excellent, it's almost a requirement for anyone who wants to be happy and everyone who wants to make the world a happier place. You don't need to take my word for it. Eric Barker, writing for *Time* magazine's *Guide to Happiness*, listed "Gratitude, Gratitude, Gratitude" first, saying, "I can't emphasize this one enough. Showing gratitude for the good things you have is the most powerful happiness boosting activity there is."[1]

Former Surgeon General Vivek Murthy notes gratitude as a key strategy for longevity and health. Murthy says gratitude is powerful because, along with meditation and strong relationships, "it creates a greater sense of emotional well being, which then gives [people] the fuel and the energy, if you will, to ... make changes in their lives and in their community."[2]

It's important to note that gratitude is an ongoing activity, a journey. It's an *attitude of gratitude*, not a set number of thank-you's and then we're done. If we want to be happy, we can never check gratitude off the "to-do" list.

One of the strongest advocates for gratitude is Dr. Robert Emmons, who has been called the world's leading scientific expert on gratitude. In his tiny but mighty *Little Book of Gratitude*, Emmons takes a deep spiritual dive into the heart of the matter. He writes,

> Gratitude is not just good medicine, ... a warm
> fuzzy feeling, or a strategy or tactic for being hap-
> pier or healthier. It is also the truest approach to
> life. We did not create or fashion ourselves, and
> we did not get to where we are in life by our-
> selves. So living in gratitude is living in truth. It
> is the most accurate and honest approach to life.[3]

Living in gratitude is living in truth—an accurate, honest
approach to life that rings true to my experience of Unitarian
Universalist goals. I suspect many other spiritual practices
and religious beliefs embrace a similar philosophy.

One unexpectedly powerful way to appreciate just how
much our lives depend on others is to consider a piece of
chocolate. In the meditation classes I lead, I hand out small
chocolate bars and ask everyone to consider, how were the
cocoa beans grown? By whom? With what help from the
rain, the soil, the sun, even the tiny midges who pollinate the
trees?[4] Who harvested the beans? Packed them for shipping?
Trucked and loaded them on cargo boats? Who cooked for
the workers on that boat? Unloaded the beans and took them
to a factory? Who created the recipe and packaging for this
particular chocolate bar? The chocolate makers? The company's marketing and sales force? Who stocked the grocery
store shelves, and made it possible to buy the chocolate and
deliver it to you? You can go even deeper with these questions
but the lesson is clear: to have even one small chocolate bar
to eat is a minor miracle.

The same is true for almost everything else we enjoy
and generally take for granted in our lives. Roads. Books.
Crayons. Living in gratitude is indeed living in truth.

Perhaps because it *is* truth, gratitude can also be comforting, like a good friend stopping by to help in times of need. That is why I often choose to lead a guided gratitude meditation class during times of collective distress, like yet another mass shooting. In such times, many of us feel down and dark at the beginning of our session. After meditating on gratitude for thirty to forty minutes, almost miraculously, we are calmer, hopeful, and much more aware of all that is good in our lives.

Gratitude also thrives in happy times. Emmons suggests the gratitude we feel on celebratory occasions moves us toward greater engagement and stronger participation in the moments of our own lives. This leads to greater positivity, which in turn builds more personal thriving, resilience, creativity, and optimism.

In an article for *Greater Good Magazine*, Emmons explains that gratitude "blocks toxic, negative emotions" and that "grateful people have a higher sense of self-worth ... because when you're grateful, you have the sense that someone else is looking out for you...." Further, Emmons shares research that shows gratitude makes us more helpful, generous, compassionate, forgiving, and outgoing, as well as less lonely and isolated.[5]

Clearly, gratitude offers a myriad of benefits that lead to greater physical, emotional and even spiritual well-being. But that is not all gratitude can do. Importantly, it can help us to climb off the hedonic treadmill—the natural human tendency to adapt, to good or bad, and then to want more of the perceived good.[6] While sometimes useful, the hedonic treadmill can, ironically, detract from pleasure and lead to wasteful consumerism or a sense of meaninglessness. Because the treadmill is based on adaptation, it is constantly pushing us in the direction of dissatisfaction with *everything* in our lives.

Say, you marry the most wonderful person in the world. As time goes on, maybe you start feeling a little less satisfied with your wonderful partner. And this might then cause you to start to wonder if you could do better. Or, more prosaic, you get a new set of plush towels. Before long, you decide it's time for *another* set of new towels, even more plush, or in a newer, more exciting color—whether or not you need them and can afford them. Either way, as with countless other coveted relationships and acquisitions, the initial high inevitably fades. Unless we are mindful, the hedonic treadmill will always have us wanting more—more shopping, more highs— because we have adapted, and are thus no longer quite as appreciative of what we already have.

But when we see with eyes of gratitude, we can limit the incessant wanting. We can refresh our enjoyment and love for the spouse and the towels. The treadmill would have us yearning for greener pastures, while gratitude empowers us to instead be thankful for, and take pleasure in, our own plot of earth.

Brother David Steindl-Rast, a Benedictine monk and an internationally admired gratitude and spiritual leader, makes the connection between the hedonic treadmill, gratitude, and happiness. He states, "Gratefulness is the key to a happy life that we hold in our hands, because if we are not grateful, then no matter how much we have we will not be happy—because we will always want to have something else or something more."[7]

Piero Ferrucci agrees. He writes, "Some people seem to have had everything in life but are not content because they do not see the value of what they have and concentrate on what they still would like, or on what makes them unhappy. Others, instead, maybe less fortunate, appreciate simple things that many of us take for granted—good health, a fine day, a smile."[8]

"The possibility of feeling grateful," says Ferrucci, "is open to us in every moment of our life."

I suggest we seize these moments! It can make all the difference. During a recent mammogram, I was struggling to tamp down feelings of anxiety. My mother and her mother died from breast cancer. Naturally I wonder if I am next. While I waited for the technician, I tried gratitude as a coping strategy—gratitude for the imaging machinery that now exists, for the kind technician, for access to health care. This may sound outlandish, but the truth is, that simple shift turned an uncomfortable necessity into a moment of beauty.

Gratitude can be powerful! An attitude of gratitude can bestow incredible benefits, if you make it a regular part of your life. That takes time and attention, just like cultivating mindfulness or staying on track with a meditation practice.

Matthieu Ricard, the Dalai Lama's French interpreter, makes the comparison between meditation and watering a plant: you need to do both regularly.[9] You can't leave a plant in a corner all month long with no water, and then shower it for an hour and expect it to thrive. The same is true for gratitude. Our souls are thirsty all month long.

Emmons cautions, "the grateful state of mind, as accessible as it is, can be fleeting, difficult to sustain over the long haul unless practised with attention and intention. So we need to immerse ourselves in practices and techniques that will foster gratitude every day."[10]

There are many ways to do this—for example, keeping a daily gratitude journal. I started my first gratitude journal on January 23, 1998. One entry was, "I'm grateful to have provided 'the biggest ray of sunshine all year' to the sno-cone lady." I have no idea what that means, though it must have been a lovely interaction. My final entries were on January 28th, just five days later. I was grateful for rice pudding and a local public radio host.

Fortunately, my husband Bob and I stumbled upon another long-lasting gratitude practice. Every evening at dinner, we raise our glasses in an appreciative toast to some-one or something. This can range from getting a new pair of winter boots, to the joy of noticing blueberries ripening in the garden, to saluting one of our children's accomplishments. Or, it could be a bittersweet toast to a loved one who is suffer-ing, or even someone who recently passed away. We've been sharing a moment of gratitude almost every single night for at least fifteen years.

Here's another version: one of my friends says out loud three things for which she is grateful *after* she finishes dinner each evening. She says this practice never fails to uplift her, no matter how challenging her day was.

Sometimes I journal, too, along with other practices. But my favorite was painting a monthly watercolor of gratitude. This practice made me get out my watercolors, which I don't do nearly enough, and led me to think about gratitude all month long as I pondered what would rise to the top of the list to be my next painting. Some of my painting choices were: yoga (I did a crude sketch of downward facing dog); the word, "words", oh so colorfully; and the trees the neigh-bor behind us planted years ago, now tall enough to give both households much more privacy.

You can also write gratitude letters, and deliver or read them to the recipient, though you don't have to if that's uncomfortable. Or you can make gratitude a regular part of your meditation practice (another favorite of mine). One friend has an online "virtual jar" for her friends to share their gratitude. I like the virtual jar idea because when I read what everyone else is grateful for, it helps illuminate new and different ways for me to be grateful, too. You can be creative and make this practice your own. Just be sure to devote significant time and heart.

Time is *very important* because, according to neuropsychologist and well-being expert Rick Hanson, "For most people, most beneficial experiences have no lasting value."[11] What Hanson is referring to is neuroplasticity, that wonderful capacity our brains have to rewire in a more positive way. The problem is, positive experiences are not as readily installed in our brains as negative experiences which, historically, could have life-threatening consequences. If, however, we give positive experiences enough time and consideration, they can become embedded in our brains, with long-term benefits for our health and well-being.

Through the "magic" of neuroplasticity, we *can* grow inner strengths such as compassion, kindness, and gratitude, but we simply must give these concepts and experiences enough time to take hold. We need to really lean into the grateful moment, savor it, feel it with our hearts, and, if possible, make it a more fully embodied experience (possibly through writing, art, or dancing). Hanson's teachings suggest that absorbing gratitude in this deeper, more thoughtful way will help rewire our brains so that gratitude becomes part of who we are on a daily basis.

This actually *is* brain science, but that doesn't mean it's hard to do. Here's one way I took Hanson's advice to heart: I used to quickly dash off a list of five things in my gratitude journal. Now, I take my time, writing much more extensive entries, trying to feel all the feelings, with a list of only three gratitudes. Quality over quantity!

Installing gratitude as a trait in our hearts and minds can have a big payoff. You've likely heard of post-traumatic stress, but may be less familiar with post-traumatic growth, a kind of benefit or improvement that can also occur after trauma. This is yet another happiness nugget I learned from Tal Ben-Shahar who explains:

> Post-traumatic growth comes when we ... actively look for a meaning in what had just happened to us. It comes when we share our experiences, when we open up rather than close down.... It's possible for many more people who have gone through trauma, who have gone through difficult experiences to experience growth as a result.[12]

For me, that growth came a few years ago in the form of greater gratitude. Thanks to an attitude of gratitude, I believe I experienced post-traumatic growth after being treated for my potentially blinding retinal condition—to be clear, a treatment that involves getting needle injections in the eye. The treatment terrified me, as did the knowledge that I came so close to losing my eyesight. But what I now remember are all the blessings I received then. I still feel a warm glow. Gratitude made the whole episode much more positive and that episode, in turn, made me a more grateful person overall.

Recently, I watched my friend Cliff moving through the same cycle. He had blown out his Achilles tendon and was immobilized, so some of us got together to take a dinner party to him. Cliff, a very athletic person, was facing months of inactivity, yet he kept coming back to everything he's grateful for. Cliff believes that gratitude helped him heal faster, because his pleasure in feeling grateful for incremental improvements helped mobilize him to continue improving. These days, he's back on the ski slopes and deeply grateful for his full recovery.

Cliff's personal story is backed up by science. According to Emmons, "in the face of serious trauma, adversity, and suffering, if people have a grateful disposition, they'll recover more quickly." Further, "gratitude gives people a perspective from which they can interpret negative life events and help [sic] them guard against post-traumatic stress and lasting anxiety."[13]

Of course, gratitude and struggle can live side by side, something that Steindl-Rast, also an Austrian survivor of World War II, knows all too well. He says, "not for everything that's given to you can you really be grateful. You can't be grateful for war in a given situation, or violence, or sickness, things like that. So the key, when people ask, 'Can you be grateful for everything?' —no, not for everything, but in every moment."[14]

In every moment, gratitude is a choice—a choice that can make us happier and better people. Not that it is always easy, of course. Some moments in life are straight up grim. Perhaps in those moments, Oliver Sacks' perspective may be inspiring. In the famed neurosurgeon's final book, *Gratitude*, which was published posthumously, he wrote:

> I cannot pretend I am without fear. But my predominant feeling is one of gratitude. I have loved and been loved; I have been given much and I

have given something in return; I have read and traveled and thought and written. I have had an intercourse with the world, the special intercourse of writers and readers. Above all, I have been a sentient being, a thinking animal, on this beautiful planet, and that in itself has been an enormous privilege and adventure.[15]

Despite the science and beautiful words penned about gratitude, there's been a backlash against embracing it wholeheartedly. *Greater Good Magazine* responded to the critics who say gratitude is self-indulgent, selfish, and breeds acceptance of the status quo rather than fueling an urge to work for improvement. Researchers Christina N. Armenta and Sonja Lyubomirsky ask, "Does gratitude lead to complacency? Do all those benefits of gratitude come at a price—laziness, apathy, and the acceptance of inequities?"[16]

You'll be glad to know—but not surprised—that their answer is a resounding "no." Based on two decades of research, including some of their own, the two women say gratitude is "an activating, energizing force that may lead us to pursue our goals and become better, more socially engaged people."

To understand how and why gratitude makes us better, in the article Armenta and Lyubomirsky identify four distinct gratitude pathways:

Connectedness. "We believe that feeling grateful compels us to reflect on our relationships and leads us to feel closer and more connected to others," they write. "Feeling close and connected to others may motivate us to improve ourselves and become better people because we want to prove that we are worthy of our relationships and because we feel encouraged, supported, and inspired by the people in our lives."

Elevation, that "warmth in one's chest and feeling moved to be a better person." They write, "We believe that gratitude makes people feel elevated—which then bolsters their motivation and effort toward self-improvement."

Humility, which matters, according to the authors, because "expressing gratitude takes the focus off of ourselves and forces us to recognize that our successes are due, at least in part, to the actions of other people."

Indebtedness may not be a pleasant feeling. Nonetheless, Lyubomirsky and Armenta write, "Reflecting on how much people have helped us may lead us to feel obligated to repay them for their help, uncomfortable because we needed help in the first place, and guilty for not thanking them sooner." This mixture can lead to "positive action" and can, in turn, increase "motivation, competence, and confidence towards self-improvement."

Cultivating gratitude may even help bring us closer to world peace, thanks to the connection we feel with others when we are grateful to them, even if they are far removed from our daily lives, like rice farmers in India. According to Dr. Kerry Howells, gratitude researcher and teacher at the University of Tasmania, "Such a sense of interconnectedness ... moves us out of our individualism and separateness and towards a recognition of our absolute dependence on others." She adds:

> At the core of most wars and atrocities is the resentment we hold in our hearts. Our reflection on how we could do things differently next time, not only steers us back towards gratitude and personal integrity, but is a crucial step towards world peace.... Our own gratitude can make a difference.[17]

Chapter Eleven

But some days, we're not interested in self-improvement, much less world peace. Sometimes, we're just trying to make it through the day—like the time I had to spend a day at a holiday co-op in a mall, selling my leftover watercolor crafts. I had agreed to be part of this venture, but when the day of my volunteer shift arrived, I was so grumpy and resentful that my daughter said, "Mom. You need to change your attitude." I agreed, and decided to do that by focusing on gratitude.

It was easy to be grateful driving to the mall, thanks to the beautiful Green Mountains surrounding the interstate. Once my shift started, I was determined to find something about each individual for which I could be grateful. And, because we see what we're looking for, I found it. Something in everyone inspired gratitude.

By the end of the day, I was quite happy. My gratitude cup was full. For that day, that was more than enough. For each day, may you also find ways, large and small, to fill your gratitude cup.

May it be so.

Reading, Writing, Social Justice— and Happiness

First Universalist Church and Society of Barnard
July 7, 2019

The more that you read, the more things you will know. The more that you learn, the more places you'll go.

—Dr. Seuss
Oh, the Places You'll Go! (1960)

The winter of 2019 was rough in Vermont. Most people seemed to struggle more than usual. For many of us, it wasn't just the weather, which delivered piles upon piles of snow. My own challenge stemmed from my husband Bob's absence. Our daughter, a single mom teaching university students in Wisconsin during the days, needed extra help with childcare while she directed those students at night in a production of *Urinetown*. Bob's retired, so off he went—for six long weeks, from late January through early March.

I often joke that whenever Bob leaves, everything mechanical in our house takes a vacation. This time the phone broke.

The bedroom heater went cold. I couldn't drain the bathtub. A massive ice cap hung menacingly from the porch roof and it became too dangerous for me to use the front door. Taking out the trash was like climbing Mt. Everest, with hard-packed snow and ice making every step a struggle. One night while coming home from choir practice, I got stuck in a snowbank and had to call AAA's roadside service. I'm sure there was more; I've just repressed it.

Plus, I missed Bob, of course.

Now, on top of all the trouble, February and March are not my favorite time of year. A friend of mine calls those two months, *"Farch!!"* (said with great disgust). So I tried my regular happiness practices. I tried gratitude, exercise, and meditation. I'm sure they helped. I think.

But what really made the difference was Spanish. Si, es verdad! Yes, it's true. Learning Spanish made *Farch!!* bearable ... even happy.

You see, I was preparing to be a presenter at the 2019 Gross Global Happiness gathering in Costa Rica in March—a trip I could only afford thanks to generous GoFundMe donors. They motivated me to do my very best. A crash course in Spanish was part of that effort.

Every day, I studied for dos horas (two hours) using Duolingo online, as well as the Pimsleur method which we have on tape. While others griped about the weather, I was deeply engrossed in learning.

My friend Marilyn made it through winter in a similar fashion. After a lifetime of being told she couldn't sing, she signed up for voice lessons. On our rides to and from the gym, she excitedly shared her singing stories. I replied in Spanish.

Learning, it turns out, is a pathway to happiness. The question is, why? I no longer remember the source, but I once read, "We [humans] have big brains and we like to use them."

I do remember where and when I first read that learning is key to happiness. It was 2009. In my early days of trying to understand the Gross National Happiness framework, I visited the website of a British organization, the New Economics Foundation (NEF). The NEF's 2008 Mental Capital and Wellbeing Project was tasked by the government's Foresight initiative "to develop a long-term vision for maximising mental capital and wellbeing in the UK for the benefits of society and the individual."[1]

From their research, the NEF developed five keys to wellbeing: give, take notice, be active, connect, and keep learning. For learning they suggest, "Try something new. Rediscover an old interest. Sign up for that course. Take on a different responsibility at work. Fix a bike. Learn to play an instrument or how to cook your favourite food. Set a challenge you enjoy achieving. Learning new things will make you more confident as well as being fun."[2]

Theirs was the first of many happiness lists I have since seen, and it's about the only one which mentions learning. Sonja Lyubomirsky does exhort people to, as she puts it, "Learn until the day you die—be it barbecuing, Spanish, knitting, the history of World War II, an effective way to maintain friendships, a new word game, etc."[3] But she frames the learning more as a strategy for achieving *flow*, admittedly a very desirable state, rather than learning for its own sake.

The only other place I've seen a spotlight on learning as a happiness tool was on the website of a particularly wonderful British organization called Action for Happiness. This group is more grassroots-oriented, a self-described "movement of people committed to building a happier and more caring society … [to create] a fundamentally different way of life—where people care less about what they can get just for themselves and more about the happiness of others."[4] Action for Happiness doubled the New Economics Foundation's five happiness keys to ten keys, including learning. Learning, or what they call *Trying Out*, "affects our well-being in lots of positive ways. It exposes us to new ideas and helps us stay curious and engaged. It also gives us a sense of accomplishment and helps boost our self-confidence and resilience."[5]

I'm not a researcher, but I find myself wondering why learning is *not* front and center of the happiness movement. I think, for example, of how exciting my mediation graduate school learning was, and how much happier the world would be if everyone learned what I now know about conflict resolution. Of course, that's just a slice. There's so much to learn! Learning about diversity, learning how eating less meat is better for the planet, learning how to grow tomatoes, learning how to grow kids, and learning how to grow old—all along the way, learning seems to be a fundamentally important tool for well-being.

Social scientist Margaret Wheatley takes my wondering to a whole new level when she emphasizes the crucial importance of learning for both individuals and organizations. "Individuals and teams who engage in learning are much more innovative, engaged, and work well together in trusted relationships. Without question. We know this," she writes. "I admit that every time I've spoken about the need to bring learning from experience back into organizational decision-making, I've felt ridiculous. Really?! We don't know this is essential to our survival? C'mon people …"[6]

The need to keep learning applies to all organizations—including the mini-one that each of us embodies, our own personal system. Learning is essential to our own survival; it deserves the spotlight of our attention. As Wheatley puts it, "When thinking falters, a living system is at risk. If it continues unchecked, the organism dies. Think about it."

That is a powerful motivator for continuing to learn. Perhaps we know that instinctually, on some level, which is one reason many of us seek out inspirational speakers, in church and elsewhere—not just to be inspired, but to learn. And then, to be inspired by *what* we learn.

But these days we don't even have to leave home to access incredible learning tools. I was first introduced to the New Economics Foundation in the comfort of my own room, watching economist Nic Marks on the TED stage. Many times since, I've tuned into his TED talk explaining the Happy Planet Index. I never thought I'd be so drawn in by an economist, but I was an immediate fan of the Happy Planet Index, which considers each country's carbon footprint as part of determining overall happiness. Costa Rica, with high levels of happiness and a relatively low carbon footprint, tops the Index by a wide margin.[7]

Marks' TED talk has received over two million views. It inspired me so much that I bought a book by another economist, Mark Anielski, a Canadian who published *The Economics of Happiness: Building Genuine Wealth*. I read passages from Anielski's book aloud to my husband in the car on a long road trip. Good thing Bob's a lifelong learner, even about economics.

Here's something else I've noticed about learning: one thing can lead to another. The first ever Gross National Happiness conference in the US, a gathering focused on systems change, was held in 2010. There, panelist Susan Andrews, founder of the Future Vision Institute in Brazil, opened my eyes to the science of personal happiness. That learning has been transformative for my own life, as well as for so many students and readers through the years. Like an Olympic torch, I am passing the learning forward.

Conferences are a superb learning tool, but a bit too costly and distant, perhaps, for many of us to attend on a regular basis. On the other end of the spectrum, there are plenty of free online courses. And let us not forget libraries and books! I have piles of books beside my bed. I read at the beach, in the tub, under the covers, in front of the wood stove, even to a baby. Contemporary writer Rebecca Solnit describes the magic of books in *A Velocity of Being: Letters to a Young Reader*:

> Some books are toolkits you take up to fix things, from the most practical to the most mysterious, from your house to your heart, or to make things, from cakes to ships. Some books are wings. Some are horses that run away with you. Some are parties to which you are invited, full of friends who are there even when you have no friends. In some books you meet one remarkable person; in others a whole group or even a culture. Some books are medicine, bitter but clarifying. Some books are puzzles, mazes, tangles, jungles. Some long books are journeys, and at the end you are not the same person you were at the beginning. Some are hand-held lights you can shine on almost anything.[8]

Solnit's love letter could easily be sent to most adults I know. It reinforces for us bibliophiles just why we continue to love books so passionately in the Internet era. Her description of the power of books would surely make many a grown-up heart soar, and cause readers of all ages to grab the nearest book. Learning need not always be the goal; many of us treasure reading's capacity to help us temporarily escape reality. Still, even in escapist reading—for example, Alexander McCall Smith's series on lady detectives in Botswana—I learn a lot. And I love that about reading.

With books, the Internet, and lectures, we can actively seek out learning opportunities. Sometimes though, whether we like it or not, the learning comes to us, unsought and perhaps unwanted. When we pay attention, life itself is one of our best teachers. This poignant paragraph from *family friendpoems.com* sums up this kind of unasked-for learning:

> It has been said that life is the most patient teacher. You will be presented with the same experience over and over until you learn the best way to deal with the situation. This is not because life is cruel. Rather, it is because things have a way of coming back to haunt us when we don't deal with them. One form of intelligence is the ability to learn from mistakes. When you are presented with a painful experience, take the time to think about how you can avoid it in the future. This is an example of a lesson learned.[9]

Perhaps you've felt, as I sometimes do, a desire to cry out to the universe, "Thanks, but I've learned enough now!" We all know it doesn't work that way. Life's hard lessons may not seem very happy-making in the short run, but if they prevent long-term suffering—if we can, in some way, grow from them—then these episodes can contribute to our well-being.

How we choose to use our learning is key. We can decide to learn something *just because*. My friend Anita recently posted a photo on Facebook from a two-and-a-half-hour wine and cheese class she took in Paris. "Here is what I learned," she said. "French Brie is to American Brie what English cheddar is to Kraft singles ... in other words, two very different things!" That sounds pretty happy-making to me, no matter how Anita chooses to apply or not apply that knowledge to her "real" life in California.

However, it is often the case that we can, and should, put our learning to use.

I've pondered the affirmation we recite weekly in unison at the Unitarian Church of Montpelier. It includes these words: "Love is the doctrine of this church, the quest for truth is its sacrament, and service is its prayer." In other words, learning is a sacred duty. And putting that learning into action through service is also a sacred duty.

For example, my GNHUSA colleagues have spent a lot of time collecting data on what makes people happy. That's great. But I want to put that data to use. What good is the learning without taking action? On the other hand, how valuable is action without the underlying data to help determine the wisest course to take? Learning and service: they make a powerful team.

Of course, not all learning is as enjoyable as surveying people about happiness. During a recent long drive, Bob and I listened to a deeply disturbing book: *These Truths: A History of the United States*, by Jill Lepore. We all know that history can be a horror show. Here in America, the double sins of stealing land from and slaughtering Indigenous people along with enslaving millions of Africans made for a really disturbing, painful listening experience as we drove. At one point, I had to turn the book off because I was crying, which is not advisable for a driver going sixty-five miles an hour on a crowded interstate.

It wasn't easy, but I felt duty-bound to continue this learning. How can we solve today's problems if we don't know how we got here? We know that white supremacy wasn't born during the Trump administration, but we should be clear on its origins, then decide what to do about it—real solutions, lasting solutions.

Probably most of you have never heard of Benjamin Lay. In 2017, a *Smithsonian* article called Lay a "Quaker Comet" and the "greatest abolitionist you've never heard of."[10] Lepore introduced me to Lay, and to the uneasy fact that even Quakers didn't readily embrace abolition.

Lay was a very unpopular Quaker due to his early and relentless opposition of slavery. Lepore describes an episode when Lay hollowed out a book, filled it with pokeberry juice, then took that book to a Quaker meeting house. There, because the Quakers still supported slavery, Lay made a big show of stabbing the book so the "blood" spurted everywhere as he decried the evils of slavery.[11]

According to the *Smithsonian* article, at another Quaker meeting, his fiery words got him kicked out of the building, so he just lay down in the mud in front of the door so everyone exiting the building had to step over him.

Lay wasn't all spectacle. He was also a passionate writer who further aroused Quaker fury in 1737 with his book, *All Slave-Keepers That Keep the Innocent in Bondage, Apostates Pretending to Lay Claim to the Pure & Holy Christian Religion; Of What Congregation So Ever; But Especially in Their Ministers* (published, interestingly, by Benjamin Franklin).[12] Lay walked his talk. He was a vegetarian and made his own clothes because he refused to contribute to an animal's death or use anything made by slave labor. He also lived in a cave.

Toward the end of his life, when Lay had been officially

disowned by the Quakers, that religious community began the process of, eventually, fully condemning slavery. Lepore's book made it sound as though Lay's efforts were critical to the Quakers' shift, and thus to the abolitionist movement. I hope so.

Thank you, learning. Unexpectedly, I found a new hero.

Here's another hero I found somewhat unexpectedly: Harriet Tubman. I've known the name "Harriet Tubman" since childhood, but I didn't know much about her until our church choir performed "They Called Her Moses," a six-movement cantata by Robert De Cormier with narration woven throughout about Tubman's life.

The music inspired me to learn more, and that's the unexpected piece. I turned once again to a book, *Harriet Tubman: The Road to Freedom* by Catherine Clinton. Like Benjamin Lay, Harriet Tubman was an incredible person. Her safe rescues of hundreds of slaves seem almost superhuman.

But we shouldn't let her daunting achievements stop us from following in her footsteps. Tubman steadfastly did her extraordinarily dangerous work—literally step by step—for decades before the Civil War and the Emancipation Proclamation. She had no way of knowing when or if the slaves would be freed. Still, she kept at it. And kept at it.

As must we. Keep at it. Surely the monumental, imperative challenge of shifting to an economy capable of living in harmony with nature and each other is as great an undertaking as ending slavery. Learning is our sacrament. It is our sacred duty to understand what we need to do. And service is our prayer, following the lead of Benjamin Lay and Harriet Tubman, step upon tenacious step.

May it be so.

When Mother Nature Ain't Happy

First Universalist Church and Society of Barnard
July 21, 2019

> *Sooner or later, we will have to recognize*
> *that the Earth has rights, too, to live without*
> *pollution. What mankind must know is that*
> *human beings cannot live without Mother*
> *Earth, but the planet can live without humans.*
> —EVO MORALES
> *"Bolivia's Defiant Leader Sets Radical*
> *Tone at Cancún Climate Talks,"*
> *The Guardian, December 11, 2010*

I have three personal stories to share. The first is about an experience which I hope you've also had—not exactly like mine, but a similar euphoric connection with nature. The second, I hope hasn't happened to you, but I fear it probably has, in some form. The third story took place in Costa Rica, but it could just as easily happen any place with a welcoming forest nearby.

Let's begin with a camping trip to Vermont's Knight Island in northern Lake Champlain. Knight Island State Park has just seven primitive, isolated camping sites. There, you can go a whole weekend without seeing or hearing other humans. There are no bridges or ferries to the island. You could try arriving by kayak or canoe, but the waters can get rough enough to swamp smaller boats. That actually happened to a young couple while we were there. They lost all their camping equipment and supplies.

We weren't that adventurous. Our party of five hired a motorboat service. The pilot dropped us off on Friday afternoon and promised to pick us up sometime on Monday.

The campsites have no electricity or running water. There are lean-tos, composting toilets, an occasional snake, acres of trees and wildflowers, piles of rocks, a handful of cliffs, miles of restless lake water, and—almost the entire time we were there—a tenacious, howling wind. To which we added fire, carefully tended in the fire pit.

Thus, with some additions, like coloring books and coffee, we spent three days and nights immersed in all the elements of nature: earth, air, water, fire. I can't imagine a better setup for meditating, which I did every afternoon. By day three, the meditation experience was transcendental. The wind, the rocks, the water, me ... we were all one. I was no longer separate from nature. I *was* nature. It was a moment of profound connection.

That is an experience I hope each of you also know, and perhaps, if you are fortunate, have felt many times.

Story number two, on the other hand, takes a turn into the gloomier aspects of our relationship with nature. Hang in there with me—it will get sunnier again in a few pages.

This nature encounter gone awry happened one Thanksgiving in Racine, Wisconsin. My daughter's apartment is just a short stroll from a brand-new boardwalk that winds down through freshly planted native grasses to a small beach on Lake Michigan. There's something romantic about boardwalks, even on a raw November day. The reeds and grasses were so lovely as I wound around the loop down to the sand ... which I was dismayed to discover was covered in trash—mostly plastic. I hate litter, but this was worse than litter. The trail was new, but the plastic was aged. That meant the trash had washed up on shore from the waters of the lake.

On a sunny day, Lake Michigan's blue-green waters rival the tropics for beauty. It was sickening to witness the truth that this gem, this unquestionably great lake, was filled with garbage. What in the world have we done to nature? What are we doing to ourselves?

I went online for some answers and happened upon the Alliance for the Great Lakes. In an article about plastic pollution in the Great Lakes, the Alliance reports:

> More than 22 million pounds of plastic pollution end up in the Great Lakes every year, according to the Rochester Institute of Technology. And, it never really goes away. Instead it just breaks down into smaller and smaller pieces known as "microplastics." ... Researchers have found stunningly high amounts of tiny plastic pieces in all five Great Lakes, which provide drinking water for 40 million people. They've found microscopic pieces of plastic in drinking water, and even beer.[1]

Plastic-infested drinking water for forty million people. Including my daughter and granddaughter.

Despite this grim news, we humans are taking some positive steps. The Alliance points to a 2015 federal ban on plastic microbeads, and also invites participation in their Adopt-a-Beach program which involves 15,000 volunteers every year, on hundreds of beaches, removing eighteen tons of trash annually. That's a lot of people using a lot of muscles to take care of our natural resources.

When it comes to humans and nature, there are many encouraging developments. *Positive News* recently reported that England budgeted ten million pounds to plant more than 130,000 trees. British environmental secretary Michael Gove said, "We need trees lining the streets of our cities and towns, not only to green and shade them but to ensure that we remain connected to the wonders of the natural world and the health and wellbeing benefits that it brings us."[2]

But, as always, there is discouraging news as well. For instance, birds.

A paid feature by the organization Allbirds in the *New York Times*' "The View From Above," notes that, "As the canary in the coal mine metaphor suggests, when the birds are in trouble, so are we." In the article, David Yarnold, president of the National Audubon Society, explains, "Birds need what people need, such as clean water, healthy forests and resilient coastlines."

The article notes that birds are plant pollinators, dispersers of seeds, and they eat "between 400 million and 500 million metric tons of insects a year globally, reducing the need for pesticides." They also "perform the role of garbage disposal by devouring animal carcasses that would otherwise rot." Unfortunately, in part due to climate change, "five North American species are particularly threatened. The Painted Redstart, Scarlet Tanager, Pygmy Nuthatch, Allen's Hummingbird and Mountain Bluebird...."[3]

Hummingbirds? Bluebirds? Scarlet Tanagers? All threatened? That's decidedly bad.

Obviously, humans have the capacity to do both dreadful harm and great good for nature. The question is, what will it take to tip the scales in favor of respect for, restoration of, and reunion with nature?

I'd like to believe that love is the answer. It may seem a naïve or radical concept in a world so heavily influenced by monetized systems of accountability to say that love is the answer. I'd prefer to think of it as a practical solution. Under a GNH paradigm that values nature, at least as much as money, our hearts would be free to once again fully embrace nature and recognize it as something we are part of, rather than separate from. Our love might then motivate us to protect and heal Mother Nature to our own great benefit, since nature truly is the mother of us all.

The kind of love I'm talking about is clear-eyed. Nature brings us trilliums, a wild orchid that blooms in spring on the forest floor, and it brings us poison ivy. Nature offers ladybugs, and ticks. It delivers vibrant rainbows and fiercely destructive hurricanes. In other words, it's a package deal.

I'm advocating a healthy love: living in harmony with nature rather than trying to control it. Controlling nature might seem ingenious for the short term, but what are the long-term ramifications?

In a surprisingly gripping book called *The Control of Nature*, well-known American writer John McPhee explains that, over time, the natural course of the Mississippi River would shift the waterway about an hour west to join up with the Atchafalaya River. This would seriously conflict with the surrounding cities, factories, and other treasured aspects of human culture built around the Mississippi's current path.

Thus, for nearly a century the Army Corps of Engineers has fought to control the Mississippi, to keep it where it is. McPhee says their defeat is inevitable. Nature will prevail.[4] And then, imagine the suffering.

Back in the early twentieth century, essayist John Crowe Ransom beautifully articulated this misguided belief that human dominion can and even *should* somehow conquer nature: "Ambitious men fight, first of all, against nature; they propose to put nature under their heel; this is the dream of scientists burrowing in their cells, and then of the industrial men who beg of their secret knowledge and go out to trouble the earth."[5]

What Ransom describes is clearly *not* a loving relationship. Nor, as nature is showing us with ever greater ferocity, is it at all practical to keep trying to bend nature to do our bidding. Love is a much more reasonable solution, even, perhaps, an easy one. Margaret Renkl, author of *Late Migrations: A Natural History of Love and Loss*, started 2020 by publishing an op-ed in the *New York Times* called "Effortless Environmentalism" featuring "easy ways to live more gently on earth." One of Renkl's "easy ways" spoke to the importance and power of loving nature, *all* of nature:

> The best thing you can do to save the earth is to fall in love with your own world. When you love something, you want to nurture and protect it. It's lovely to think of preserving the earth as a matter of protecting the oceans and the forests and the flood plains and the prairies. But preserving the earth is just as much about protecting the blue jays and the spiders and bats and the garter snakes and the box turtles and the toads.

Pay attention to their courtship songs and their territorial cries of fury. Study their stirring in the leaves. Listen for the rush of wings.[6]

It is an understatement to say that Mother Nature isn't feeling enough love from humans, and, indeed, is not very happy with us. Remember the adage, "If Mother Nature ain't happy, ain't nobody happy"? Painful evidence of this truth is all around us: an abused nature appears to be lashing back at humankind. Every day, it seems, the term "record breaking" is tied to stories of drought, heat, floods, and hurricanes. However, the Happiness Alliance, a project in Seattle, Washington, which has been collecting and analyzing well-being data nationwide since 2012, suggested in an email newsletter that we should turn the equation around: "Mother Nature plus human nature [can] equal happiness."[7]

The Alliance analyzed data from eleven thousand people in their 2018 Happiness Index, comparing "how happy people are when they are satisfied with their opportunities to enjoy nature versus when they are dissatisfied with their opportunities to enjoy nature."[8]

The results? People who are satisfied with their opportunities to enjoy nature may gain 25 percent more happiness and tend to have a significantly greater sense of belonging to community. Their sense of purpose and meaning, a crucial happiness measure, is 28 percent higher, and they have 21.9 percent more satisfaction in their lives.

A couple of considerations stand out from their analysis. An Environmental Protection Agency study, quoted in a *Time* magazine article on forest bathing, found that "the average American spends 93% of his or her time indoors."[9] That leaves only 7 percent, then, that apparently is spent outside.

Now, many people may feel quite satisfied spending so much time indoors; I have a hard time convincing my granddaughter to come play outside with me on a Wisconsin winter day. Nonetheless, Americans as a whole do not seem to be deriving enough happiness benefits from nature.

They may also be missing the greater sense of belonging and purpose derived from satisfying experiences with nature—a deeper commitment to the environment that comes from shifts within the heart and soul. Knowing that we don't want to drink plastic and that trees can help combat climate change is intellectual, "in-the-head" knowing. But spending so much time indoors may be robbing us of the chance to form a more powerful, heart-based connection with nature.

One way to reverse this trend is through forest bathing, a series of guided exercises in the woods to help participants become more mindful of, and connected to, the natural world. Forest bathing is also called shinrin-yoku in Japan, where the ancient practice was revived in the 1980s to help highly-stressed Japanese workers. At least, that's what forest therapy guide Manuela Siegfried told the group I was part of in Costa Rica. The Association of Nature and Forest Therapy Guides and Programs lists some wonderful benefits of forest bathing:

- "Improved mood and feelings of health and robustness," thanks to the physicality of long walks in the woods;
- Decreased levels of the stress hormone cortisol;
- Lower stress levels;
- "Increased parasympathetic nervous system activity which prompts rest, conserves energy, and slows down the heart rate;"

- A boost in immune functioning;
- Greater creativity; and
- Possibly even some anti-cancer benefits.[10]

The bottom line is that spending quality time in the woods is healing. We just feel better—in mind, body, and spirit. Yes, there are bugs and briars, and the occasional intimidating animal, but in the hands of a good guide, anyone can safely and happily navigate an afternoon in the wild. Which leads me to the third story I wanted to share.

In the Costa Rican forest, the month of March is the tail end of the dry season, and so my forest bathing experience was, for me, unexpectedly brown and crunchy rather than green and lush. Still, I loved it, and had three reactions:

First, gratitude. In the opening exercise, as we began our trek into the woods, we were instructed to share nature memories with a partner. I told my partner about Knight Island, and of a childhood spent playing in the creek and woods behind my Pennsylvania house. Her experience was quite different. Her father, she said, had defined camping as staying in a hotel without room service. Even now, living in densely populated Tokyo, she yearns for more nature in her life.

Thus my gratitude: in Vermont, I enjoy ready access to nature. There are hiking trails right out my back door. Further, I am acutely aware that forest bathing, in general, whether in Vermont or Costa Rica, is a happiness privilege that so many lack access to. This makes me sad. Under a Gross National Happiness paradigm—which values both protecting nature and ensuring that individuals have more personal time at their disposal—perhaps many more people would be enabled to enjoy nature and benefit from her gifts.

My second reaction to forest bathing in Costa Rica was awe. For about ten minutes, our guide had us stand with eyes closed, using our other senses to become more finely attuned to our surroundings. Just before we opened our eyes, we were instructed to imagine that whatever we saw was looking right back at us. My eyes landed on a large bush with many petite green leaves—all of them, seemingly, looking at me! I cannot explain what happened, but, like my experience on Knight Island, the illusion I carry in day-to-day life of separation between me and the rest of nature temporarily dissolved.

This kind of reverence may well be good for mental health. *Greater Good Magazine*, for example, reports on a study led by social and personality psychologist Craig Anderson. He says, "You don't have to do extravagant, extraordinary experiences in nature to feel awe or to get benefits ... By taking a few minutes to enjoy flowers that are blooming or a sunset in your day-to-day life, you also improve your well-being."[11] That's terrific news! Even those without easy access to the forest or other more expansive natural surroundings can still benefit, regularly, by being mindful of nature's more quiet offerings.

Nature's benefits aren't just psychological or spiritual—there are down and dirty ways that nature makes us happier. Literally. There are microbes and bacteria in dirt that have an anti-depression effect on the brain. The microbes, *mycobacterium vaccae*, actually mimic the effect of serotonin.[12] Not surprisingly then, gardening is quite beneficial. It may even help us live longer. Dan Buettner, who researches what he calls "Blue Zones"—places where people live the longest—says moderate physical activity and spending time outdoors are linked to longer lives.[13] With gardening, you get both.

Maybe just being in gardens is helpful. In his book *Everything in Its Place*, neurologist Oliver Sacks wrote:

> I take my patients to gardens whenever possible. All of us have had the experience of wandering through a lush garden or a timeless desert, walking by a river or an ocean, or climbing a mountain and finding ourselves simultaneously calmed and reinvigorated, engaged in mind, refreshed in body and spirit. The importance of these physiological states on individual and community health is fundamental and wide-ranging.[14]

There are many articles out there extolling the benefits of nature. One observation I appreciated was from researcher Andrew Weil. He says, "As part of our evolutionary heritage, human beings—both children and adults—have a profound need for time in wild, outdoor spaces, and we suffer when we don't get it."[15]

Indeed, for everyone with children in their lives, it is important to get them outside, too. *Psychology Today* reports that "Low Childhood Nature Exposure is Associated with Worse Mental Health in Adulthood."[16] Journalist Richard Louv, author of *Last Child in the Woods* and other books, warns us of "nature-deficit disorder," especially among children. In an interview with Jill Suttie in *Greater Good Magazine*, Louv explains that this disorder,

> ... is not a medical diagnosis, but a useful term—a metaphor—to describe what many of us believe are the human costs of alienation from nature: diminished use of the senses, attention difficulties,

higher rates of physical and emotional illnesses, a rising rate of myopia, child and adult obesity, Vitamin D deficiency, and other maladies.[17]

Louv goes on to stress how important it is to love nature, for children to have experiences that implant nature in their hearts as well as their heads:

> If nature experiences continue to fade from the current generation of young people, and the next, and the ones to follow, where will future stewards of the earth come from? Past research has shown that adults who identify themselves as environmentalists or conservationists almost always had some transcendent experiences in the natural world. What happens if that *personal* experience virtually disappears? There will always be conservationists and environmentalists, but if we don't turn this trend around, they'll increasingly carry nature in their briefcases, not in their hearts. And that's a very different relationship.

I certainly worry about the world my granddaughter will inherit. I know many, many others feel the same way about the children in their lives. I want her to be happy, and to have the best possible tools to protect and nurture the natural world she will inherit. Thanks, in part, to the summers she spends with us in Vermont where we climb mountains, swim in the pond, and search for toads, she does now carry nature (even slugs!) in her heart. I want her, and all of your beloved young ones as well, to continue to love nature. This will help ensure a more liveable and joyous future for everyone.

One of the best ways to help kids, then, is to love nature ourselves and actively model that love. Thus I know that my forest bathing experience, however I choose to share it with my granddaughter, will also benefit her—because it deepened my love for nature, she will see that in me.

Now for one last story, the third of my three reactions to my Costa Rican experience: an intense appreciation for the "Gifts of the Forest." That was the name of one of our activities, in which we were instructed to find "gifts" in the forest for our partners, who sat with closed eyes and open hands. The receiver, with eyes shut the entire time, was to take all the time she wanted to explore each offering.

Choosing the gifts, and placing them in my friend's hands, was lovely. Receiving them, though, was profound. I received an interestingly shaped twig, a withered berry, and various leaves. Each item was absolutely precious, especially the leaf that was soft and fuzzy on one side and raspy like sandpaper on the other side. The memory of that little present, which I left behind on the forest floor that day, continues to warm my heart.

I had no need to bring the leaf with me, because nature overflows with gifts for us all, from fuzzy leaves to sparkling lakes, greater health, and longer lives. The question really is, how can we best give back to nature? Can we love nature the way she deserves? I believe, if we open our doors to go outside and open our hearts to the amazing natural world that we are, in fact, part of, and if we open our minds to creating a new economic paradigm that truly appreciates the value of nature for our collective well-being, then we can do it. We can love nature, and be loved in return.

May it be so.

The Extraordinary Value of Everyday Beauty

First Universalist Church and Society of Barnard
August 4, 2019

In that moment I saw that ... beauty is not optional but a strategy for survival.... Beauty feeds a different kind of hunger.... Finding beauty in a broken world is acknowledging that beauty leads us to our deepest and highest selves. It inspires us. We have an innate desire for grace.
—TERRY TEMPEST WILLIAMS
Finding Beauty in a Broken World (2008)

One summery Saturday morning, I pulled a beautiful shawl from a cardboard box across the street. The box was part of a massive free pile—table after table laden with treasures from my friend Mandy's life. Mandy loved nature, children, and beauty, so there were animals in all shapes, sizes, and textures, from books to bubble blowers. Children's toys, delicate napkins, and the prettiest of notecards. I chose the shawl to remember Mandy, who died when she just could not handle any more pain and took matters into her own hands.

I knew about Mandy's lifelong struggles, and I was aware that both children and nature were safe refuges for her, but I didn't realize how much beauty mattered to Mandy until her memorial service. For her, beauty was healing, a balm to her battered soul. Whether it was the spectacular patterns of frost on a winter window, or a carefully color-coordinated outfit, Mandy sought out everyday beauty like a sunflower leans toward the sun.

Mandy may have carried more pain than most, but, just as all flowers need the sun, all humans need beauty. Piero Ferrucci, whose book on kindness is like a happiness bible for me, has written another invaluable text: *Beauty and the Soul: The Extraordinary Power of Everyday Beauty to Heal Your Life*. Ferrucci insists that beauty, far from being frivolous, is a primal need. "Beauty," he writes, "is not like a distant satellite, but like a sun that gives life and light to all areas of our life."[1]

Ferrucci's statement comes after years of immersion on the topic, including studying and teaching beauty, conducting interviews about its effects on people, and drawing observations from his psychotherapy work. Over time, he says, "I increasingly saw the extraordinary effects of beauty on our personality." The subjects he interviewed shared many different reactions to beauty: "'I forget all my fears,' 'I understand so many things,' 'I glimpse happiness,' 'I feel relieved and fulfilled,' 'I am grateful to be alive.'"

We can do a little research ourselves, here and now. I invite you to close your eyes and remember a moment of beauty you've experienced. It doesn't have to be extraordinary, though it can be. Anything from a wildflower poking up through the cement to first touching a new baby's toes. Music, or a painting. Maybe a gesture, or a poem. Any beautiful moment will do. When you've found one to sit with, try to drink it all in—all the textures, colors, aromas, and sounds—to make the experience in this moment as full-bodied as possible.

Do you feel how that beautiful moment, even now, is feeding you and nurturing you? Does it make you smile? Are you suffused with love, gratitude, or perhaps contentment?

In any case, I imagine it feels good. Life affirming.

Now, try to imagine: there is no longer any beauty. No colors, no beautiful words; no music, no seascapes. No beauty at all. Anywhere.

I'm sure that idea arouses much more negative emotions. I can't even do this second part of the exercise. A life without beauty is just too bleak to comprehend. We may not need beauty the same way we need air, water, and food—that is, to exist at all. But I wonder, without beauty, would life be worth living?

Fortunately, as the famous Navajo prayer "Walking in Beauty" makes abundantly clear, we are surrounded by beauty. The Unitarian Universalist hymnal contains a version of this timeless blessing which reminds us, "Beauty is before me, and Beauty behind me, above me and below me hovers the beautiful ... I am immersed in it.... In beauty it is begun. In beauty, it is ended."[2]

"Seek Not Afar for Beauty," a song from the same hymnal, underscores the point that life overflows with ordinary, everyday beauty: "Seek not afar for beauty; lo, it glows in dew-wet grasses all about your feet, in birds, in sunshine, childish faces sweet, in stars and mountain summits topped with snows."[3]

Beauty is frequently there for us when we need a lift. Many times, it is free, ready to elevate and heal us up when we have the mindfulness to genuinely see and connect with it.

There are also times when the beauty is neither ordinary nor possible to ignore. That happened to me one memorable evening, at a time when my spirits definitely needed some lifting up. I was driving a rental car alone through the Florida panhandle wilderness, not at all confident that I was headed in the right direction. I had been sick the night before and had slept very little. With ginger ale, crackers, and willpower, I had pulled myself together enough to get to the rental agency in Tampa where I refused to buy extra insurance on the car. Now, in the wilderness, still a little shaky, maybe lost, I was increasingly worried about wrecking the car, or worse. I was close to panicking.

Yet high above me was a wildly spectacular sunset. The sky in all directions was alive with vivid pinks, purples, oranges, reds, and blues. It was surreal. I hung onto that sunset like a life raft—until darkness closed in. I was still two long hours away from my destination. That was plenty of time to slightly wreck the car by running over a curb (which I did do). The sunset didn't solve all my problems, but it temporarily eased my troubled mind. I can still conjure it up whenever I want, just by closing my eyes.

Beauty clearly matters. Yet, I believe its true importance in our lives is given short shrift, on both the personal and policymaking levels. While there is some consideration for beauty in, say, national parks, beauty doesn't show up in the most commonly used metric about our collective well-being, the Gross Domestic Product. As Bobby Kennedy observed back in 1968, the GDP measures everything but that which makes life worth living—like beauty.[4] Nor do policymakers who propose selling off public lands seem concerned about access to beauty for all citizens, regardless of income. Even the Gross National Happiness system so far neglects the importance of beauty. But GNH measurements are still being developed in the US and worldwide—maybe beauty will get more notice.

On a personal level, I suspect most of us enjoy beauty quite a lot. Still, I doubt it is in many people's calculations of what they want to achieve each day. My own daily checksheet includes gratitude, kindness, and meditation but "taking in the beauty" hasn't made the cut so far. I'm really just waking up to the value of everyday beauty in my own life.

Positive psychology, on the other hand, has long noted that beauty is crucial to well-being. Indeed, the capacity to appreciate beauty is one of positive psychology's twenty-four universally admired character strengths—which surprised me. I get that love, forgiveness, emotional intelligence and other such obviously noble qualities are on the list. But beauty? Clearly, there is more to beauty than I realized.

According to the VIA Institute on Character, those who rank high as appreciators of beauty and excellence, "notice and appreciate beauty, excellence and/or skilled performance in all domains of life, from nature to art to mathematics to science to everyday experience." The VIA says the benefits can include feeling energized and elevated, as well as having a desire to be better, a sense of awe and wonder, and admiration.[5]

At the same time, beauty has a dark side—like obsessions to possess art masterpieces and hide them away, or to collect beautiful people as personal trophies, or to monopolize natural vistas for one's personal enjoyment of nature.

Then there's the omnipresent pressure to be personally beautiful, which exacts a horrifying toll exemplified by eating disorders, body shaming, and billions spent on cosmetics. An article in *The Atlantic*, "The Beauty-Happiness Connection," shared a Yale study which made me cringe because it concluded "that being beautiful adds to one's overall life happiness … [because] prettier people tend to make more money, and it is this financial leg up that affords beautiful people great happiness."[6]

That's how we see beauty? As a way to make more money?

The pressure to be beautiful is interwoven in our culture in so many ways, including how we compliment children. I've met many parents who push back against the way their young daughters are constantly being lauded as "so pretty!" as if that is what matters most about the girls. Yet even for such diligent parents, I think the beauty bias is so pervasive, it's sometimes invisible. I once attended a family concert featuring a soprano whose voice is the very definition of beauty. She sang a delightful version of the "Ugly Duckling." I enjoyed her performance until I suddenly heard what the story was all about. In this version, even the duckling's mother abandons her child because it isn't beautiful enough. All the creatures pick on the ugly duckling until, amazingly, it transforms into a beautiful swan. Then, *voila!* The animals are all in awe of the physically transformed bird. Sorry to be a killjoy, but this is NOT a fun story. The duckling is never valued for its inner beauty. And worse, the ugly duckling is black, while the beautiful swan is white.

One look at Hollywood's leading ladies and gents provides strong evidence that our society prefers to see beautiful *white* people on the screen. This preference may be shifting, at least internationally. In December 2019, the *New York Times* reported that all five major international beauty pageants—including Miss USA and Miss America—had most recently been won by black women.[7] I'm not a big fan of beauty contests, but that seems to indicate a growing diversification in beauty ideals.

Not only beauty standards but also access to everyday beauty are likely limited by race. *Greater Good Magazine* republished a 2005 article by Jonathan Kozol called "Schools Without Beauty." Kozol discusses inner city schools where, he says, "the insult to aesthetics, the affront to cleanliness and harmony and sweetness, are continuing realities ... for children who must go each morning into morbid-looking buildings in which few adults other than their teachers would agree to work day after day." In one elementary school, Kozol observed:

> The principal poured out his feelings to me in a room in which a plastic garbage bag had been attached somehow to cover part of the collapsing ceiling. "This," he told me, pointing to the garbage bag, then gesturing around him at the other indications of decay and disrepair ... "would not happen to white children."[8]

"There is no misery index for the children of apartheid education," Kozol says, but "There ought to be; we measure almost every other aspect of the lives they lead in school. Do kids who go to schools like these enjoy the days they spend in them? Is school, for most of them, a happy place to be?" I think we all know the answer to that.

I don't doubt for a moment that children of color are all too often steered into schools in need of serious repair and fresh paint jobs, but I don't think they are the only kids treated this way. A teacher friend of mine says the same is true of small-town schools, rural schools, and poor schools. She's seen the same kinds of problems Kozol writes about: missing ceiling tiles, mold, water leaking on teacher's desks, classrooms with no windows and not much heat. The teachers' rooms in these schools, too, she says, are filthy and dingy. Perhaps it's affluent school districts that are set apart.

Before Irish poet and priest John O'Donohue's death in 2008, he told public radio's *On Being* host Krista Tippett "that an awful lot of urban planning, particularly in poor areas, has doubly impoverished the poor by the ugliness which surrounds them." Yet, O'Donohue notes, "It's not just a matter of the outer presence of the landscape ... the dawn goes up, and the twilight comes, even in the most roughest inner-city place." He suggests, "If you can keep some kind of little contour [of beauty] that you can glimpse sideways at, now and again, you can endure great bleakness."[9]

I love O'Donohue's devotion to beauty, and his priestly and poetic insights. At the same time, isn't that asking a lot of our children? To endure the bleakness of their schools by glimpsing sideways at beauty within?

I think we all know the answer to that, too.

The good news is that beauty's dark side is not actually the fault of beauty itself. The warped views of beauty and the neglect are man-made constructs and we can reject them.

Take the Navajo, for instance. They have an entirely different perspective on beauty—the concept of *hózhó*. Recently I learned more about the context for the "Walking in Beauty" prayer on a website called *Design for Peace: Practices for Sustaining Lives of Meaning, Joy, and Beauty*. According to Jen Wolfe's blog, originally published in *Southwest Legends*, "Perhaps the most important word and concept in the belief system of the Navajo people is hózhó." This word roughly translates to mean: "to be in balance and beauty with the world." Wolfe further explains, "It is about health, long life, happiness, wisdom, knowledge, harmony, with both the mundane and the divine. It means a traditional Navajo person is continually restoring, finding, and practicing balance in his or her daily life."[10]

She says, "the concept of hózhó sounds simple, but it isn't. For instance, while other Native American tribes pray for rain during a drought, the Navajo hold ceremonies to put them in balance and harmony with the drought." She concludes, "Hózhó ought to be the goal of humanity as it is the goal of holy people of the Navajo Nation."

I don't want to misinterpret either the Navajo or Piero Ferrucci, but perhaps Ferrucci is suggesting something similar when he writes:

> In this amazing and frightening era, institutions are losing their force and can no longer help us. The values of justice, freedom, and love are becoming abstract and distant, outshone by the lure of a thousand seductive promises. In such a critical situation, beauty can be a lifesaver – because it is all around us, if we know how to find it. It is beyond any dogma. It is immediate and spontaneous. It can be the way back to ourselves.[11]

My Gross National Happiness colleague John de Graaf—the man who coined the term *affluenza*—has recently shifted his focus to beauty. He is one of the founders of And Beauty for All, an organization which, according to its website, is devoted to "bringing Americans together and healing our wounds by embracing natural beauty and human design in ways that revitalize our communities and renew our environment."[12]

In a 2019 speech, de Graaf said, "In spite of its great wealth, its growing economy and its low unemployment rate, America is unhappy, angry, and polarized to a degree I cannot remember in my entire 72 years on this planet." He suggested that only a sense of shared values, like beauty, can "fully soothe the ill will or smooth out the conflict."[13]

De Graaf's group seems philosophically aligned with both the Navajo and Ferrucci, but his organization is more focused on public policy. De Graaf mulls over public policies that could make America more beautiful, and more united. A few of his ideas include mountaintop restoration, eliminating billboards, the Green New Deal, a national mural project, a small farm support act, and local home beautification grants.

He's right. So much can be done, on the outside, creating more healing beauty across the country. Across many countries. Each of us can better advocate for and benefit from public policy advancements that promote beauty in homes, neighborhoods, parks, public lands, classrooms, and shopping areas. We can do this by working together, but also individually by cultivating a greater internal awareness and appreciation of beauty as a key contributor to our happiness.

In my research on beauty, it was an unexpected pleasure to learn that neuropsychologist Rick Hanson recommends exactly that—cultivating our relationship with beauty for greater happiness. He says beauty "actually changes the brain. It alters brain wave patterns when we do respond to something as beautiful, taking us to a place of relaxation, as well as happiness." That beauty, he says, is everywhere, even inside of us. He urges, "See if you can find even some of the beauty inside yourself and when you do … give yourself over to it.... Even the breath, the breath is beautiful. You can breathe in beauty, and you can let beauty breathe you."[14]

Like mindfulness, like time in nature, like so much of our lives, experiencing beauty need not be grand to be powerful, to be healing, or to make us happy. We need only look around. For example, right here, right now—what do you see in this moment that is beautiful? If you don't see anything beautiful in your immediate surroundings, can you appreciate what is beautiful within you? Or perhaps, a memory, or a place you will be going to where there is beauty, something as simple as a beloved teapot on a worn but favorite tablecloth?

Yes, we can work to enhance and preserve beauty for the happiness of all. At the same time, the extraordinary value of everyday beauty is there for each of us, just as the sun is there for sunflowers.

May you all have a beautiful week.

May it be so.

Creativity: Save the Planet, Produce a Masterpiece, or Just Have Fun

First Universalist Church and Society of Barnard
August 11, 2019

Q. What is creativity? A. The relationship between a human being and the mysteries of inspiration.

—ELIZABETH GILBERT
Big Magic: Creative Living Beyond Fear (2015)

In 2019, I developed a new relationship with rocks. With some exceptions, I used to barely notice them; rocks were just extended dirt. Now, I look down while I walk, scouring the ground for rocks to become canvasses for mini-paintings. I choose rocks for their smoothness, or the designs in the rock formation that I want to highlight with my paintbrush. Rocks are now partners in my creative process.

This relationship with rocks actually started in 2011–2012, the brief time when I created and managed the Happiness Paradigm Store and Experience. I decided to demonstrate the value of kindness and generosity by giving each person who stopped by an ordinary, vaguely heart-shaped stone, each adorned by a glittery heart I painted on the rough surface. I am still kind of amazed at how much these heart rocks meant to so many people. Just a little rock, picked up out of the dirt!

When I closed the store, I stopped painting rocks until we began camping on Lake Champlain. The lake's shores are strewn with a seemingly infinite supply of black and brown stones (Iberville shale), each with its own unique white markings (veins of a mineral known as calcite).[1] In particular, the straight-ish white streaks cutting through many of the rocks look to me like birch trees in need of painted foliage, grass, and cheery blue skies. I colored the first set of trees with pastels borrowed from a fellow camper. After that, I bought some cheap acrylics and brushes, found just the right rocks to stuff in my pockets, and began my birch tree series. I've since added more experimental hearts and other abstracts, where I give myself permission to just go with the flow and see what happens.

I paint rocks because it makes me happy. There's no goal, no bottom line involved. This is creativity for its own sake. It is an escape from deadlines, headlines, budgets, and commitment. Painting rocks is fun.

Creativity does not need to be, and often is not, any bigger than that. Like beauty, it can be ordinary, a kind of elevated playtime. On the other end of the spectrum, creativity can give rise to masterpieces, like the US Constitution, Monet's water lily paintings, the poetry of Maya Angelou, or Lin-Manuel Miranda's Broadway rap-musicals.

Creativity can also guide us through daily life, with new answers to questions like, "Given the strange assortment of items in my fridge, what should I make for dinner tonight?"

Or, when your toddler is melting down in a crowded public space, "How shall I handle *this*?"

There's more. Not only is creativity crucial in devising and implementing solutions to the world's problems, it can also help us to better face reality, hang tough, and return again and again to the emotional and physical challenges of confronting current injustices and building a happier, sustainable future.

One of my friends and fellow activists, for example, uses a large collection of colored sharpies to help her work through her rage and sorrow about issues like children locked in cages by the US government near the border with Mexico. She draws and colors images from the depths of her heart as therapy. It helps her continue to protest (even in the rain), write letter after letter, and fundraise for lawyers on the front lines.

Creativity works the same magic for me. After a few hours of rock painting, I can get back to the never-ending demands of movement organizing—hosting public education films and discussions, calling members of Congress, knocking on doors to get out the vote, and composing email after email with my fellow organizers. It is *much* easier to do this work when my spirits are high, or, at least, steady.

Creativity is a shape-shifter: large, small, serious, frivolous, a balm to the soul, or a nudge from one's muse. Even trying to define creativity is elusive. Michael Grybko, a neuroscientist from the University of Washington, says, "In science, we define 'creativity' as an idea that is novel, good, and useful."[2] The website *Creativity at Work* emphasizes the act rather than the idea: "If you have ideas but don't act on them, you are imaginative but not creative."[3]

Here are a few more definitions from various authors:

- Creativity is "the ability to connect the seemingly unconnected and meld existing knowledge into new insight about some element of how the world works."[4]

- "Creativity is harnessing universality and making it flow through your eyes."[5]

- "[Creativity is] just making something. It might be something crummy or awkward or not ready for prime time. If you make something, you are creative."[6]

So is creativity just making stuff, or is it the harvesting of universality? Whatever it is, it is an essential part of being a happy human. As journalist Brenda Ueland put it, "There is nothing that makes people so generous, joyful, lively, bold and compassionate, so indifferent to fighting and the accumulation of money" as using our creative power.[7]

Sadly, many people don't realize that they have an innate ability to be creative. All too often during my craft show years, I heard people say, "I don't have a creative bone in my body." Perhaps that's because they conflate creativity with being artistic, or believe that creativity is an elusive quality visited only upon "creative types." Or maybe creativity doesn't live in the bones!

Though my craft show customers may not have believed me when I said that yes, they too were creative, human history is a saga of regular people being creative: designing and building homes, creating their own clothes, inventing new recipes as they grew and prepared food, crafting their ornamentation and children's toys. Creativity is a birthright.

Or as author Elizabeth Gilbert puts it in *Big Magic*:

> If you're alive, you're a creative person. You and I
> and everyone you know are descended from tens
> of thousands of years of makers. Decorators, tin-
> kerers, storytellers, dancers, explorers, fiddlers,
> drummers, builders, growers, problem-solvers and
> embellishers— these are our common ancestors.[8]

No wonder Dieter Uchtdorf, a leading figure in the
Church of Jesus Christ of Latter-Day Saints, says, "The desire
to create is one of the deepest yearnings of the human soul."[9]

Sometimes, our creative endeavors can take us to the
highly desirable state of flow—that sense of the world falling away and time disappearing while you paint, or com-
pose, or garden. Hungarian-American positive psychologist
Mihaly Csikszentmihalyi, who has built a career around
studying the creative process, suggests that the ecstatic state
of flow is *the key* to happiness. He describes flow as "being
completely involved in an activity for its own sake. The ego
falls away. Time flies. Every action, movement, and thought
follows inevitably from the previous one, like playing jazz.
Your whole being is involved, and you're using your skills
to the utmost."[10]

I've certainly experienced that happy state of flow. When
images for paintings come to me, and I try to bring them to
life, I feel the creative force flowing through my arm and hand
onto the paper. Perhaps that is the ego falling away. It certainly feels like I am channeling from some source other than
my own brain. Time does fly. I just want to paint, and paint,
and paint. Quite unusually for me, I don't even care that much
about eating. I agree that flow is a pretty sweet spot.

Which brings us to perhaps the biggest question about creativity: Where does it come from? These images for paintings—technically, I suppose they are my ideas, but it doesn't feel that way. From my experience as a writer, painter, and facilitator of creativity retreats, as well as from the opinions of experts in the field, it seems clear: the creative process is both practicality and mystery, both a scientific and spiritual undertaking. It is often hard to locate, definitively, the source or origin of creative inspiration.

There are, however, steps that we can take to respond better to inspiration, and see our creative projects through to fruition.

Dancer, choreographer, and creativity expert Twyla Tharp says, we need to do the work. "Creativity is a habit, and the best creativity is a result of good work habits," she writes. "That's it in a nutshell."[11]

Michael Grybko offers another pragmatic perspective:

> Pooling from this wealth of knowledge we store in our brains and making connections between different ideas, we have to solve a new problem, or create, write a new novel ... Just to drive home the point, this is very much a function of the brain. There's no need to invoke all that folklore into this. It's our brains doing what they do.[12]

And though Csikszentmihalyi's descriptions of flow sound mysterious and spiritual, he boils it all down to science in his TED talk. He explains that flow occurs because the human nervous system is capable of handling only a limited amount of stimulation at any given time, and that when one is fully focused on a creative activity, the nervous system simply isn't capable of attending to anything else—like time passing away.

Csikszentmihalyi has a formula for getting to this peak happiness state. His flow formula includes concentrating completely on the task at hand, being clear on goals, and striking a balance between your skill level and the difficulty of the task. That is, if what you are trying to do is either too easy or too hard, you won't experience flow.[13]

I've never tried to follow Csikszentmihalyi's advice; I've just fallen into flow on my own. I have, however, used the work of Dr. Robert Epstein and Roger von Oech as part of my creativity retreat teachings.

What I find most valuable about Epstein's work is his Generative Theory, which has four strategies: 1) capturing the idea; 2) challenging, or learning from failure; 3) broadening and diversifying your knowledge base; and 4) varying your surroundings, meaning changing up your external stimuli.[14] Epstein stresses that, "Creativity is an orderly and predictable process" which "means that creativity can be engineered—and that all of us can realize the enormous creative potential lying within us."[15]

It is quite wonderful, indeed, to identify a formula to help *everyone* tap into their creative potential. Part of me nonetheless chafes at this formulaic packaging of a spiritual mystery, but truthfully, it's very helpful, especially capturing. For example, I found myself writing the beauty sermon in my head while I jogged on the treadmill. The ideas piled up, more than my brain could retain for long. So as soon as I got off, I grabbed my phone and typed a long email to myself. Otherwise, all that good thinking could have drifted off to the land of escaped ideas. Creativity doesn't always show up at the most convenient times. Thank goodness for capturing!

I'm also fond of changing surroundings to encourage creativity. We scheduled our creativity retreats, in the middle of winter, at warm, sunny beach locales. However, I'm not sure this is exactly the kind of stimuli Epstein meant. He suggests visiting hospitals, or other places way outside our comfort zones. But I have to say, the beach was very stimulating!

Roger von Oech provided my other core retreat teaching in his deceptively light-hearted book *A Whack on the Side of the Head*. His helpful contribution was outlining the four roles we need to play at different stages of the creative process: the explorer who learns, broadens, and sows the seeds for creative thinking; the artist, who actively puts the pieces together; the judge, who evaluates and discerns; and the warrior, who hangs in there with the sometimes challenging work of taking ideas to the finish line.[16]

The warrior is the most helpful role for me to bear in mind. It's one thing to start writing a book, or form an organization, or have a baby, but there's an awful lot of tenacity called for between start and finish. I have trouble finishing art projects sometimes, so it is good for me to honor the inner warrior who perseveres to the end.

Elizabeth Gilbert knows all about habits and hard work, yet she also believes in the mystery and the magic of creativity. In *Big Magic*, Gilbert reports on the multiple magical experiences described by various artists. She suggests that creativity is almost a living thing. That is, ideas exist on their own. If they come to us and we actively or passively neglect them, the creative ideas will leave us in search of a more welcoming host. She says:

> The magical thinking that I use to engage with creativity is this idea that inspiration does not come *from* me, it comes *to* me. And the reason I

choose to believe that is because one, that's what it feels like, and two, that's how pretty much every human being before the Age of Enlightenment described inspiration.[17]

I read Gilbert's creativity book over Christmas vacation a few years ago. My first reaction was, this lady is way too woo-woo for me. And yet. Over and over, I have thought of how creative ideas have visited me, sometimes knocking louder and louder until I finally answered the door. How I would wake up with a life-transforming idea. How ideas spring into my head from out of the blue, in the middle of nowhere, and yet I know they are the right ideas for me.

Which is to say, I believe at least the essence of Gilbert's theory. I believe the other experts, too. I know that having an idea is one thing, but actually implementing it is another. Still, it is Gilbert's book that lives next to my pillow because she inspires me to receive creativity as a gift, and then to do my very best to make that gift welcome.

While we can't really ever know where creativity comes from, researchers can pinpoint a lot about its effect on our happiness. For example, some researchers wondered, in a chicken-and-egg kind of way: does creativity make us happy, or is it the other way around? They dug into that question, and came up with an answer.

Dr. Tamlin Conner, a psychology professor who lives in New Zealand, led a study to figure this out. In an article in *Greater Good Magazine*, Conner reports the study's results:

> People who were engaged in more creative activities than usual on one day reported increased positive emotion and flourishing the next day. [And] people

who experienced higher positive emotions on day one *weren't* more involved in creative activities on day two, suggesting that everyday creativity leads to more well-being rather than the other way around.[18]

Conner concludes, "Doing creative things today predicts improvements in well-being tomorrow. Full stop."

Another online publication, *Daily Good*, reported that creative activities "can boost your levels of serotonin and decrease anxiety." Authors Peggy Taylor and Charlie Murphy note that creativity further enhances our lives by opening "the door to the inner world of our imaginations. It is here that we make meaning of our lives. It is here that motivation takes root. The more creative we are, the more capacity we have to imagine what's possible and make those visions real."[19]

The article says there are ten things that creative people know:

1. Our lives have meaning.

2. We are all creative.

3. Creative expression empowers us.

4. We are good at heart.

5. Life is an adventure to be lived, not a problem to be solved.

6. Change is an inside job.

7. Diversity is a resource.

8. We thrive when we feel supported.

9. We each have the power to make change.

10. The challenges of our time require intergenerational collaboration.

That's quite a list! I think of myself as a creative person, yet I'm not sure I could have said I know all that, especially number ten, about intergenerational collaboration. However, number ten resonates with me for two reasons. First, when I'm participating in social justice actions, I am often pleased to see the mix of generations, co-creating justice together. Second, we simply must work together to co-create peace in these deeply troubled times.

While it's good enough to be creative for no reason other than pleasure, I am excited to see the creative solutions people are devising to solve big problems. Here are a couple of examples that make me happy:

- To encourage subway users to take the stairs instead of automatically riding the escalator, Volkswagen Sweden turned steps into giant piano keys which actually played music as people walked on them.[20] Thus, more people took the stairs because it was so much fun.

- Here in Vermont, a new enterprise called The Hitching Post has launched a Coffee Pooling system. Two restaurants at either end of a ten mile commute offer Coffee Coins. Riders purchase the coins for $1.00 each and use them to hitch a ride. Drivers giving rides can redeem the coins at either restaurant for coffee or pastries.[21] Again, a social good, carpooling, made so much more appealing in a creative, fun way!

Other creative ideas blooming across the globe include repair cafes, tool libraries, carbon sequestration, and a guaranteed annual income. My personal favorite is solar roadways. I was so excited when I first saw Solar Roadway, Inc.'s 2014 video, called *Solar FREAKIN' Roadways!*, that I lit a candle of joy at church. I understand solar roadway experiments in Idaho and France have since failed.[22] However, just the other day, I watched a video showing another solar technology in use on bike paths in Poland.[23] Ideas evolve. That's part of the creative process.

There's just one thought about creativity that gives me pause: it does not exist in a vacuum. We don't *always* have to serve humanity with our creative projects, but if we want our creativity to *sometimes* be of service, we have to nurture other qualities like mindfulness, compassion, gratitude, and love.

For example, my friend Susannah Blachly has written a devastatingly beautiful song that is definitely in service of humanity. "Colored Balloons" is a compassionate, haunting ballad about the school children in Beslan, Russia, who were murdered by terrorists.[24] Her song is a sad but outstanding example of bringing love and mindfulness to the creative process. This kind of creativity serves not only self, but also the broader community.

I have a very different way of using creativity to serve the community: I dress up my cow. When we bought our house, we inherited a large 10' by 10' painting of a cow on the front exterior, facing the street. I disliked the faded, mostly grey painting and wanted to paint over it, but I was told that it's a landmark in town. Bob and I felt social pressure to keep it. Our second Halloween here, I decided to make the best of a bad situation by painting costumes on foam board for the cow—and a community service was born. Turns out, neighbors of all ages get a kick out of seeing what the cow is wearing this month. Children, in particular, tell me how much they appreciate our cow. I have since redone the entire painting (it is so much brighter and happier), and we now have stacks of costumes. My favorite is the vacation cow—backwards baseball cap, camera slung around the neck, Hawaiian shirt and madras shorts, flip-flops, sunglasses, and a suitcase.

Susannah's song keeps the memory of those children alive in my heart, and the cow costumes offer me an opportunity to make others smile. Creativity. You never know where it might take you! I just hope you enjoy the journey.

May it be so.

Calling All Happiness Prophets: Accessing Our Sacred Instructions to Create a Better World

First Universalist Church and Society of Barnard
August 18, 2019

I have seen that community and a close relationship with the land can enrich human life beyond all comparison with material wealth or technological sophistication. I have learned that another way is possible.
—HELENA NORBERG-HODGE
Ancient Futures, Third Edition (2016)

In 2018, driving home in late November from a family Thanksgiving gathering, I heard an interview with the remarkable Sister Joan Chittister. I can picture almost where we were when the radio show started: on an upstate New York expressway, about an hour south of Albany. You know how you can sometimes remember the conditions when you first heard or saw something important? That day, the weather was greyish, but her words burst through the malaise of a long drive and darkening skies like a shining beacon. I thought, who is this woman? She is singing my song! I found a scrap of paper and wrote down her name and the radio show so I could track down this amazing interviewee when I finally got home.

The interview, it turned out, was about Chittister's newest book, *The Time Is Now: A Call to Uncommon Courage.* I immediately ordered one at my local bookstore. When it arrived, I read Chittister's description of the state we're in:

> A world gone badly askew stands on the cusp between authoritarianism and freedom, between universal compassion and national self-centeredness. It is a world scarred with violence, institutionalized fraud, rapacious human degradation, political suppression, economic slavery, and rampant narcissism. It is a world in wait. It waits for some wise and wild voices to lead us back to spiritual sanity. Our world waits for you and me, for spiritual people everywhere—to refuse to be pawns in the destruction of a global world for the sake of national self-centeredness.[1]

Chittister is calling on us all to be prophets. Becoming a prophet—which I see in secular terms as being someone who is a fiercely committed advocate for a just and loving future—seems like an appropriate choice for people of faith and good will. I say, sign me up.

Sister Joan is quite the prophet herself, a relentless voice for social justice. I don't share her Roman Catholic beliefs, but I do agree with her belief that "the time is now," for us all to "refuse to accept a moral deterioration of the present and insist on celebrating the coming of an unknown, but surely holier, future." It is time, she says in her book, "to follow the path of the prophets of old … who spoke the voice and vision of God for the world."

Since I don't really believe in God, nor do I consider a belief in God necessary to do the work of a prophet, I reinterpret Chittister's words this way: we can envision and raise our voices in support of a much happier future, where the well-being of all people, animals, and the planet is a top priority in public policies and private hearts. This is a vision well worth fighting for.

Chittister's book shares space next to my bed with *Sacred Instructions: Indigenous Wisdom for Living Spirit-Based Change,* the most recent offering from Penobscot leader and lawyer Sherri Mitchell. Mitchell, who is also known as Wch'na Ha'mu' Kwasset (She Who Brings the Light), similarly writes about the dreadful state of the world. She says it is no accident that we are now at "a critical crossroads for humanity." She continues,

> The good news is that we don't have to make this choice blindly. We have been given all the guidance that is necessary to choose the right path.... We have the capacity to create a world that is compassionately intent on preserving the integrity of all life in a harmonious balance. And that the Sacred Instructions for creating the world exist within each and every one of us right now and are waiting to be called forth.[2]

Maybe Mitchell is right. I certainly *want* to believe her. In fact, I think I do know what my sacred instructions are:

through my writing, to help build a movement for greater personal thriving and transformed systems to support well-being for all. Even if we didn't consciously choose to be here now, we *are* here now. Therefore, it is incumbent upon us to do the work, to follow our sacred instructions.

But what if people don't know what their sacred instructions are? Mitchell says, listen carefully. She explains:

> Every living being has its own vibrational tone. When these tones are combined, they form the voice of creation. If we learn to listen closely, we can begin to hear that voice and allow it to guide our steps through life. Then we can begin to attune our daily actions with our higher purpose and become who we were meant to be.

Granted, there may be times when it all feels like just too much work. It may seem more appealing and less exhausting to just get away from it all. Some of my friends talk about possibly moving to another country to escape the deteriorating democracy in the United States, but I don't see that as an option. Besides, where can anyone go? Moral deterioration and inhumane policies are widespread. A late 2019 snapshot would show a Hong Kong in turmoil; India trampling on the human rights of millions of Kashmiri citizens; Venezuela, Guatemala, and Honduras in desperate straits; even worse situations in Sudan and Syria; and a British government topsy-turvy over the separatist Brexit initiative.

If the suffering is widespread, so too are the calls for change, including warnings and solutions from happiness prophets worldwide.

Chapter Sixteen

In 2011, Italian political scientist Stefano Bartolini published a *Manifesto for Happiness: Shifting Society from Money to Well-Being*. A couple of summers ago I attended The Happiness Roundtable, a virtual international conversation, where Bartolini explained the need for this shift. For the Roundtable's website he wrote, "We live in rich countries, we have defeated mass poverty, we have access to consumer goods, education and health care and we live longer lives. However, studies on happiness in industrial countries depict a dismal portrait. Distress, mental illnesses, addictions, suicides and psychiatric drugs are on the rise in many countries."[3]

Rich countries fail on the happiness front, says Bartolini, because, "Our relationships have been sacrificed on the altar of material affluence, which knows only two imperatives: work and the consumption of material goods. Hence our increasing wealth of goods and penury of relationships. Hence our growing unhappiness."

Swedish activist Helena Norberg-Hodge, who now lives in Australia and is a founder and director of the international organization Local Futures/The Economics of Happiness, has been a prophet for well-being since the 1970s.[4] In 2019, Norberg-Hodge released a new book, *Local Is Our Future: Steps to an Economics of Happiness*. Her updated message is, "For our species to have a future, it must be local." She points out:

> The good news is that the path to such a future is already being forged. Away from the screens of the mainstream media, the crude 'bigger is better' narrative that has dominated economic thinking for centuries is being challenged by a much gen-

tler, more 'feminine', inclusive perspective that places human and ecological well-being front and center. People are coming to recognize that *connection,* both to others and to Nature herself, is the wellspring of human happiness. And every day new, inspiring initiatives are springing up that offer the potential for genuine prosperity.[5]

I had the good fortune of seeing both Norberg-Hodge and Sherri Mitchell in person as presenters at an Economics of Happiness conference in Vermont in 2017. Though I didn't get to interact with either of them personally, I was very impressed with their wisdom, love, and courage. They are bravely and doggedly sharing messages—that many in the world are not yet ready to hear—which go against the dominant cultural messages of economic growth, consumerism, and a global economy.

Their voices, and so many other prophetic voices, are putting forth bold ideas for the future while also decrying the brokenness of our current systems. Even former President Jimmy Carter has said that "the world is at a turning point in history."[6] The chorus of warnings is enough to make a person wonder, just how dire is our situation?

According to Margaret Wheatley, the crisis is extremely dire. In fact, she says, with a truckload of evidence to back her up, we are in systems collapse. In her book, *Who Do We Choose To Be?: Facing Reality, Claiming Leadership, Restoring Sanity,* Wheatley stresses that all civilizations—*all* civilizations—go through six predictable stages before falling apart. The final, sixth stage of civilization, "The Age of Decadence," is an era when:

Wealth and power have led to petty and negative behaviors, including narcissism, consumerism, materialism, nihilism, fanaticism, and high levels of frivolity. A celebrity culture worships athletes, actors, and singers. The masses are distracted by entertainment and sporting events, abandon moral restraint, shirk duties and insist on entitlements. The leaders believe they are impervious and will govern forever.[7]

Hmmm ... that sounds quite uncomfortably like the United States in 2020. Indeed, the similarity is unnerving. Yet, Wheatley acknowledges that some may "welcome in this time of disruption and chaos as the means to create healthier, more humane and life-affirming ways of living on this planet." But she cautions, "We can't get there from here without traversing the falling apart stage. We cannot simply leap to new ways of being; first we must prepare for disintegration and collapse."[8]

The potential ramifications of multiple, interconnected systems collapse—environmental, social, political, and economic—are serious, to say the least. For example, what happens if democracy collapses in the United States? Do we descend into a dictatorship?

There are red flags that this descent is already underway. In 2019, I listened to the NPR radio program *On Point* with guest Edward J. Watts, author of *Mortal Republic: How Rome Fell into Tyranny*. The parallels he describes, in the interview, between the Roman and American republics are chilling. He notes:

The thing that is particularly dangerous to look at are actions that, when they were done the first time, were seen as really aberrant and oddly sort of dangerous, that have become commonplace. Twenty-five years ago, shutting down the government for political brinkmanship was seen as absolutely crazy. It was something no one would dare do. And now it's routine. That's a sort of degeneration of norms...

The citizens of Rome took it for granted that the republic would be there. And so there were conscious choices made to either act in your own self-interest in ways that were sort of damaging to the structure of the republic and the norms that sustained it, or, if you're a regular voter, an unwillingness to punish people who behaved that way.... But the average choices individuals were making accumulated and created conditions where these norms could be violated in ways that were more subtle than marching an army on Rome, but no less destructive over a long period of time.[9]

And so Rome fell. Will the United States follow suit? In early February 2020, Neil Steinberg, a columnist for the *Chicago Sun-Times,* wrote an op-ed titled, "Crumbling US Senate Echoes Roman Collapse." He began, "In failing to hear witnesses in the trial of Donald Trump, the Senate joins other historic bodies that paved the way for despotism."[10]

Others predict the coming collapse is inevitable based on the stress our growth economy has put on the environment. But, this may ultimately be a very good development. Paul Gilding, former head of Greenpeace International, titled his 2011 book, *The Great Disruption: Why the Climate Crisis*

Will Bring On the End of Shopping and the Birth of a New World. The book jacket notes:

> We have come to the end of Economic Growth Version 1.0, a world economy based on consumption and waste, where we lived beyond the means of our planet's resources.... The coming decades will see loss, suffering, and conflict as our planetary overdraft is paid. Yet they will also bring out the best humanity can offer: compassion, innovation, resilience, and adaptability. The crisis will, inevitably, change our economic model and the way we live our lives.[11]

Ultimately, Gilding is optimistic. "We are going to have to change our expectations about our material lifestyles, about the nature and focus of our work and careers, about our expectations of government, and about how we all behave in our communities and our companies. The good news is that most of these changes are going to make us happier anyway."[12]

His long-term optimism makes me think of the Hindu god Shiva the Destroyer. Shiva is also a Creator. Perhaps the destruction of today's broken and outdated systems will make it possible for humans to create the new systems needed to support well-being for all. The future could be *better.*

Another voice of hope, Indian author Arundhati Roy, is a human rights and climate activist who says, "Another world is not only possible, she is on her way. Maybe many of us won't be here to greet her, but on a quiet day, if I listen very carefully, I can hear her breathing."[13]

When I saw Norberg-Hodge and Mitchell in 2017, they were joined by other visionaries, like Gus Speth, co-chair of the Next System Project, and Frances Moore Lappé, best known for her 1971 book, *Diet for a Small Planet*. A collective message that I heard from all the speakers was how we're in the dark times now. No one knows how dark it will get or how long it will be dark. But eventually, it will be time for the next system. No one knows what that will look like. They urged us all to keep doing our very important work to build the next system.

Their words inspire me to keep moving forward with my happiness prophecy. I do not believe in happiness alone. Indeed, it would be hubris in the extreme to think happiness has all the answers for what must be a diverse and collaborative next system. I do, however, fervently hope that part of the "What's next?" conversation will be:

1. an understanding of the implicit value of individual happiness;

2. the adoption of new, inclusive measures of success to support well-being policies planet-wide.

These are beautiful and pragmatic choices. A much happier world can be the blessing and miracle that *we ourselves cause* to arise from the dark times.

The Gross National Happiness system, which, as we've noted, proposes researching the conditions needed to support maximum happiness for all, and then making policy decisions based on *all* those conditions, is both practical and doable—once we loosen our society's obsession with measuring the GDP and making policy based only on that single, limited data set. It bears repeating: What we measure, matters. Measurements drive our behaviors. We have the power to change what we measure. We can encourage much more life-enhancing behaviors. We need only open ourselves up to the value and possibility of a GNH system.

It's a new way of thinking, but then again, as Albert Einstein said, "A new type of thinking is essential if mankind is to survive and move toward higher levels."[14]

Here's another reason to embrace and work toward the holistic vision of well-being for all beings on this planet. Martin Luther King, Jr. famously said, "Darkness cannot drive out darkness, only light can do that. Hate cannot drive out hate, only love can do that."[15] The same is true of happiness. That is, unhappiness cannot drive out unhappiness, only happiness can do that. It's common sense.

Happiness can certainly, and significantly, help us out of these dark times. The real question is, will we choose that path?

One of my happiness teachers, Maria Sirois, author of *A Short Course in Happiness After Loss (and Other Dark, Difficult Times)*, says:

> So much rests on our capacity to address two fundamental questions: Do I believe positive change is possible? Am I willing to do the work of making positive change possible? If we answer no to either question, or hold more than just a bit of doubt about either, then we are essentially choosing to continue living life as it is. But should we answer yes to each question, we have the possibility of creating life anew. Yes to both opens a doorway into a life that has its ups and downs, its sudden upheavals and its catastrophes while also offering wonder and hope and beauty and vibrant belonging.[16]

I always find Sirois a hard person to say no to, so I say, yes, yes! Let us choose happiness—for ourselves and all other beings. Let us choose hope and vibrant belonging. Together, we can create life anew.

I've talked before about one of my favorite tools for choosing happiness: learning what our character strengths are and then using them for our own well-being, as well as to do our best for others. This approach seems particularly valuable during dark, unsettled times. As Sirois once told her happiness students, in times of crises, we want to come from our strengths, not our weaknesses.

Three of the twenty-four virtues and strengths identified by positive psychologist researchers seem especially valuable these days: courage, humor, and perseverance.[17] We all have these strengths in greater and lesser degrees, and we will need to access them as prophets and builders of new systems. Here's how the VIA Institute on Character defines these three particular strengths:

- *Courage*: "I act on my convictions, and I face threats, challenges, difficulties, and pains, despite my doubts and fears."

- *Humor*: "I approach life playfully, making others laugh, and finding humor in difficult and stressful times."

- *Perseverance*: "I persist toward my goals despite obstacles, discouragements, or disappointments."[18]

Obviously, the struggles ahead will demand courage. And lord knows, we'll need all the laughs we can get! It's clear that we are confronting deeply rooted paradigms that

will be extraordinarily difficult to shift. The happiness movement can achieve great success in the world, but definitely not
without significant perseverance.

In an article in *Greater Good Magazine*, spiritual
teacher Jack Kornfield offers a useful approach for gar-
nering all three characteristics—doing our inner happiness
work:

> You ask, can changing your inner life make a
> difference in the troubles of the world? Nothing
> else can! No amount of technology, computers,
> Internet, artificial intelligence, biotech, nanotech-
> nology, or space technology is going to stop con-
> tinuing racism, warfare, environmental destruc-
> tion, and tribalism. These all have their source
> in the human heart.... The outer developments
> that are so remarkable in our human world now
> need to be matched by the inner developments
> of humanity.... This is the great task of modern
> times. To bring the inner level of human con-
> sciousness up to the level of our outer develop-
> ment. Nothing else will really make a difference.[19]

However, though personal happiness work is necessary,
it is not sufficient. When you think about school kids living
in fear that their undocumented parents will get whisked
away by government authorities, or that a gunman will shoot
them or their teachers, or if you imagine a hurricane has just
destroyed your town ... how happy can anyone be in those
circumstances? Happiness is not *just* an inside job. For systems problems, we need systems change. Fortunately, many
groups are focusing on this approach.

One such entity is the appropriately named, "Next System Project." They collaborate with a diverse group, from scientists to activists, "to promote visions, models and pathways that point to a 'next system' radically different in fundamental ways from the failed systems of the past and present and capable of delivering superior social, economic and ecological outcomes."[20] I have enormous respect for legal/environmental activist and writer Gus Speth, one of the group's co-chairs. And when I look at the rest of the team members on their website, I see a lot of brain power focused on developing a next system that will serve all of us well.

Then there is the Happiness Alliance in Seattle, Washington, led by Laura Musikanski, who, like me, is on the advisory board of GNHUSA. Through the years, I've seen Musikanski collect and analyze well-being data prolifically, and with insight. I've marveled at her stamina and production. In October 2019, Musikanski, along with Rhonda Phillips and Jean Crowder, produced another first: *The Happiness Policy Handbook: How to Make Happiness and Well-Being the Purpose of Your Government.* Now there's actually a happiness roadmap for policymakers. This movement is making progress!

One reason I am such a believer in the happiness movement is because it offers us so many wonderful ways to say *yes* in an era that will be requiring us to say no to old habits and ideas of success. *Yes* to relationships and spending quality time together; no to greed and wasteful consumerism that stresses the planet and our wallets. *Yes* to compassion and love for all beings; no to exploiting nature and animals as commodities to be used and thrown away. *Yes* to forgiveness; no to hate. *Yes* to beauty and creativity; no to overdevelopment and poisoning Earth with fossil fuels. These are our very important choices.

With happiness, we can face the future with hope. Happiness has the potential of unifying very divided societies. As Aristotle said, "Happiness is the meaning and the purpose of life, the whole aim and end of human existence."[21] That applies to all of us.

Indeed, according to Paula Francis from GNHUSA, "What truly matters in life is astonishingly consistent around the United States." She says people from all walks of life value: "Love. Kindness. Oneness. Peace. Service to others. Making others happy. Nature. And, of course, puppies!"[22]

Knowing we all want essentially the same things is a long way from creating the necessary inner and outer changes we need in order to come together and collectively heal our countries and this planet. Still, the unifying potential of collective happiness is really quite exciting. It's a place to start.

At the same time, I think so much will be required from many of us. Wheatley points to "the difficulties that lie ahead, and the frequent opportunities we will have to serve the human spirit."[23] That won't necessarily be easy. We may not wish to heed our sacred instructions. We may yearn to return to a more comfortable way of living and being, that, one could argue, no longer exists or perhaps never existed. Wheatley considers this passage from J.R.R. Tolkien's *The Fellowship of the Ring*:

> "I wish it need not have happened in my time,"
> said Frodo.
> "So do I," said Gandalf. "And so do all who
> live to see such times. But that is not for them to
> decide. All we have to decide is what to do with
> the time that is given us."[24]

I faced such a choice at the 2019 Gross Global Happiness conference in Costa Rica. Before I got there, I had been thinking that maybe this was my last hurrah, that it was time for me to retire. But I received a different message during a workshop there: My sacred instructions are to remain a happiness prophet.

The workshop, led by Jennifer Shinkai of Tokyo, featured "Ikigai," a Japanese concept for discovering one's purpose in life. She asked us three questions: What do you love? What are you good at? What can you be paid for? For each, we were asked to pick a photo that best represented our answers from her special Points of You® deck.[25]

The fourth question was, "What does the world need?" For this, the cards were face down. We couldn't see the photo until after we chose a card. I ended up with an old woman, who looked grumpy. I didn't understand why, so I put that card back (which was allowed in the rules) and picked another. It was another old woman, seemingly on holiday at a British seaside resort. This time, I kept the card. This woman's expression was puzzled, anxious, maybe a little hurt. She seemed to be pleading with me, please don't retire. Don't leave us. The world still needs you.

Somehow, I don't know how, that photo of the elderly woman conveyed my sacred instructions. I have made my choice. However enchanting or brutal these times may turn out to be, I know that I must use my life to be a prophet of true well-being, of happiness, for all. My great hope is that many of you will join with me in this cause. Together, let us create a just and joyful world.

May it be so.

Endnotes

Introduction

1. Margaret Wheatley, *Who Do We Chose to Be?: Facing Reality, Claiming Leadership, Restoring Sanity* (Oakland: Berrett-Koehler, 2017).

Chapter One: Happiness for Everyone—Our Moral Obligation to Change the Economic Paradigm

1. Annie Leonard and Jonah Sachs, "The Story of Solutions," directed by Louis Fox, The Story of Stuff Project, 2018, https://storyofstuff. org/movies/the-story-of-solutions/.

2. Martin E.P. Seligman, *Flourish: A Visionary New Understanding of Happiness and Well-Being (New York: Free Press, 2011)*, 16–20.

3. Roger J. Corless, *Vision of Buddhism: The Space Under the Tree* (St. Paul: Paragon House, 1989), 20.

4. Alexander McCall Smith, *The Right Attitude to Rain* (New York: Pantheon Books, 2006), 221.

5. OPHI, "Bhutan's Gross National Happiness Index," Oxford Poverty and Human Development Initiative, 2019, https://ophi.org. uk/policy/national-policy/gross-national-happiness-index.

6. GNH Centre Bhutan, "History of GNH," 2019, http://www.gnh centrebhutan.org/what-is-gnh/history-of-gnh/.

7. Hon. Grant Robertson, "Wellbeing of New Zealanders at the Heart of Budget Priorities," Bee.govt.nz, December 13, 2018, https://www.beeh ive.govt.nz/release/wellbeing-new-zealanders-heart-budget-priorities.

8. United Nations, "On International Day of Happiness, UN Urges Action to End Poverty, Build Harmony," *UN News*, March 20, 2014, https://news.un.org/en/story/2014/03/464252.

9. Martin Luther King, Jr., "Where Do We Go From Here: Address delivered at the Eleventh Annual SCLC Convention," The Martin Luther King, Jr. Research and Education Institute, Stanford University, accessed February 3, 2020, https://kinginstitute.stanford.

edu/king-papers/documents/where-do-we-go-here-address-delivered-eleventh-annual-sclc-convention.

10. John Adams, *The Massachusetts Constitution,* John Adams Historical Society, accessed October 11, 2019, http://www.john-adams-heritage.com/text-of-the-massachusetts-constitution/.

11. Sonya Lyubomirsky, *The How of Happiness: A New Approach to Getting the Life You Want (*New York: Penguin Books, 2007), 116.

12. Bruce Springsteen, "Badlands," track 1 on *Darkness at the Edge of Town*, Atlantic Studios and the Record Plant, 1978, CD.

13. John Green, *Looking for Alaska* (New York: Dutton Books, 2005).

14. Daniel Crockett, "Nature Connection Will Be the Next Big Human Trend," *Huffington Post,* August 22, 2014, https://www.huffington post.co.uk/daniel-crockett/nature-connection-will-be-the-next-big-human-trend_b_5698267.html.

15. Francis X. Rocca, "Pope Francis Says Ills of Global Economy, Not Islam, Inspire Terrorism," *The Wall Street Journal*, August 1, 2016, https://www.wsj.com/articles/pope-francis-urges-poles-to-embrace-migrants-on-final-day-of-visit-1469963264.

16. Pope Francis quoted in "Speech on the Poor and Indigenous Peoples," *Time,* July 10, 2015, https://time.com/3952885/pope-francis-bolivia-poverty-speech-transcript/.

17. James Gustave Speth, *The Bridge at the Edge of the World: Capitalism, the Environment, and Crossing from Crisis to Sustainability* (New Haven: Yale University Press, 2008).

Chapter Two: Happiness Runs in a Circular Motion

1. Donovan, "Happiness Runs," track 4 on *Barabajagal*, Olympic Studios, 1969, LP.

2. "Golda Meir Sayings and Quotes," Wise Old Sayings, 2020, http://www.wiseoldsayings.com/authors/golda-meir-quotes/.

3. Eric Weiner, "Bhutan's Dark Secret to Happiness,"BBC Travel, April 8, 2015, http://www.bbc.com/travel/story/20150408-bhutans-dark-secret-to-happiness.

4. "Martin Seligman," The Pursuit of Happiness: Bringing the Science of Happiness to Life, Pursuit of Happiness, Inc., 2018, https://www.

pursuit-of-happiness.org/history-of-happiness/martin-seligman-psychology/.

5. Tal Ben-Shahar, Certificate in Positive Psychology Program (online and in-person, Wholebeing Institute, Lenox, MA, February 2014–January 2015).

6. Ben-Shahar, Certificate in Positive Psychology Program.

7. Nisha Jackson, "Altruism: The Greater Good," OnePeak Medical, 2020, https://peakmedicalclinic.com/ask-nisha/altruism-the-greater-good/.

8. Sonja Lyubomirsky, Kennon Sheldon, and David Schkade, "Pursuing Happiness: The Architecture of Sustainable Change," *Review of General Psychology* 9 (2005): 111–31.

9. Susan Krauss Whitbourne, PhD, "Are You Ready to Take a Slice Out of the 'Happiness Pie'?" *Psychology Today*, June 4, 2019, https://www.psychologytoday.com/us/blog/fulfillment-any-age/201906/are-you-ready-take-slice-out-the-happiness-pie.

10. *Encyclopædia Britannica Online*, 2019, s.v. "Neuroplasticity."

11. Michael Bergeisen, "The Neuroscience of Happiness," *Greater Good Magazine: Science-Based Insights for a Meaningful Life*," The Greater Good Science Center at the University of California Berkeley, September 22, 2010, https://greatergood.berkeley.edu/article/item/the_neuroscience_of_happiness.

12. Sonja Lyubomirsky, Laura King, and Ed Diener, "The Benefits of Frequent Positive Affect: Does Happiness Lead to Success?" *Psychological Bulletin*, vol. 131, no. 6, 2005, 803-855, https://www.apa.org/pubs/journals/releases/bul-1316803.pdf.

13. Anna Almendrala, "The U.S. Surgeon General Wants to Bring You Health via Happiness," *HuffPost*, December 20, 2016, https://www.huffpost.com/entry/surgeon-general-happiness-vivek-murthy_n_564f857ee4b0d4093a57c8b0.

14. Ginny Sassaman, "'True Well-Being for Animals and People' Presentation by GNHUSA Board Member Beth Allgood," Gross National Happiness USA, September 4, 2017, https://gnhusa.org/gnhusa-news/true-well-animals-people-presentation-gnhusa-board-member-beth-allgood/.

15. Christine Carter, PhD, *Raising Happiness: 10 Simple Steps for More Joyful Kids and Happier Parents* (New York: Ballantine Books Trade Paperback Edition, 2010), 5–7.

16. Rick Hanson, PhD, "The Self-Caring Pillar: Befriending Yourself," The Foundations of Well-Being, 2014, https://www.rickhanson.net/wp-content/uploads/2014/10/1-Befriending-Yourself1.pdf.

17. Bronnie Ware, "Regrets of the Dying," Bronnie Ware, 2007–2020, https://bronnieware.com/blog/regrets-of-the-dying/.

18. "We Can Complain Because Rose Bushes Have Thorns," Quote Investigator, accessed October 23, 2019, https://quoteinvestigator.com/2013/11/16/rose-thorn/.

Chapter Three: Growing Our Happiness Muscles to Build a Better World

1. Jill Suttie, "Why We Should Seek Happiness Even in Hard Times," *Greater Good Magazine: Science-Based Insights for a Meaningful Life,* The Greater Good Science Center at the University of California Berkeley, January 4, 2019, https://greatergood.berkeley.edu/article/item/why_we_should_seek_happiness_even_in_hard_times.

2. Barbara L. Fredrickson, PhD, *Positivity: Top-Notch Research Reveals the 3-to-1 Ratio That Will Change Your Life* (New York: Three Rivers Press, 2009), 21.

3. Fredrickson, *Positivity*, 23.

4. VIA, "Character Strengths," VIA Institute on Character, 2020. https://www.viacharacter.org/character-strengths-via.

5. Neal Mayerson, PhD, Embodied Positive Psychology Summit (Wholebeing Institute, Lenox, MA, April 2016).

6. Maria Sirois, email message to author, October 13, 2014.

7. Maria Sirois, Certificate in Positive Psychology Program (Wholebeing Institute, Lenox, MA, February 2014–January 2015).

8. Martin E.P. Seligman, PhD, *Learned Optimism: How to Change Your Mind and Your Life* (New York: Vintage Books, 1990), iv.

9. Seligman, *Learned Optimism,* 20.

10. Abraham H. Maslow, *Toward a Psychology of Being* (New York: John Wiley & Sons, 1968).

11. Utpal Dholakia, PhD, "4 Reasons Why An Optimistic Outlook Is Good for Your Health," *Psychology Today,* July 31, 2016, https://

www.psychologytoday.com/us/blog/the-science-behind-behavior/
201607/4-reasons-why-optimistic-outlook-is-good-your-health.

12. Seligman, *Learned Optimism*, 4–5.

13. Tal Ben-Shahar, Certificate in Positive Psychology Program (online and in-person, Wholebeing Institute, Lenox, MA, February 2014–January 2015).

14. Ben-Shahar, Certificate in Positive Psychology Program.

15. Jim Collins, *Good to Great: Why Some Companies Make the Leap ... and Others Don't* (New York: HarperCollins, 2001), 85.

16. Emily Esfahani Smith, "The Benefits of Optimism Are Real: Having a Positive Outlook is the Most Important Predictor of Resilience," *The Atlantic*, March 1, 2013, https://www.theatlantic.com/health/archive/2013/03/the-benefits-of-optimism-are-real/273306/.

17. Rick Hanson, PhD with Forrest Hanson, *Resilient: How to Grow an Unshakable Core of Calm, Strength, and Happiness* (New York: Harmony Books, 2018), 2.

18. Howard Zinn, "The Optimism of Uncertainty," *The Nation*, September 20, 2004, https://www.thenation.com/article/optimism-uncertainty/.

Chapter Four: All You Need is Love—But It's Complicated

1. The Oxford Dictionary of Difficult Words, "dogma" (Oxford UP, 2004), 138.

2. Tal Ben-Shahar, "Relationships Are the Ultimate Currency," Wholebeing Institute, 2019, https://wholebeinginstitute.com/relationships-are-the-ultimate-currency.

3. Ed Diener and Robert Biswas-Diener, *Happiness: Unlocking the Mysteries of Psychological Wealth* (Malden: Blackwell Publishing, 2008), 23.

4. Ed Diener and Martin E.P. Seligman, "Very Happy People," *Sage Journals*, January 1, 2002, https://journals.sagepub.com/doi/10.1111/1467-9280.00415.

5. Benjamin Hardy, PhD, "This 75-year Harvard Study Shows How to Have Lifetime Joy," Thrive Global, Medium.com, April 25, 2018, https://medium.com/thrive-global/this-75-year-harvard-study-reveals-the-secret-to-happiness-and-success-3cf0002510fe.

6. Neel Burton, MD, "These Are the 7 Types of Love," *Psychology Today,* June 25, 2016, https://www.psychologytoday.com/us/blog/hide-and-seek/201606/these-are-the-7-types-love.

7. Jimmy Buffett, "Fruitcakes," track 2 on *Fruitcakes,* Margaritaville Records/MCA, May 24, 1994, CD.

8. Nicholas Kristof, "Let's Wage a War on Loneliness: The Condition Isn't Just Depressing. It Can Be Deadly," *New York Times,* November 9, 2019, https://www.nytimes.com/2019/11/09/opinion/sunday/britain-loneliness-epidemic.html.

9. Bianca DiJulio, Liz Hamel, Cailey Muñana, and Mollyann Brodie, "Loneliness and Social Isolation in the United States, the United Kingdom and Japan: An International Survey," Kaiser Family Foundation, August 30, 2018, https://www.kff.org/report-section/loneliness-and-social-isolation-in-the-united-states-the-united-kingdom-and-japan-an-international-survey-introduction/.

10. Barbara L. Fredrickson, PhD, *Love 2.0: How Our Supreme Emotion Affects Everything We Feel, Think, Do and Become* (New York: Hudson Street Press, 2013), 85.

11. Rachel Naomi Remen, MD, *Kitchen Table Wisdom: Stories That Heal,* (New York: The Berkley Publishing Group, 1996), 143–144.

12. Stephen R. Covey, *The 7 Habits of Highly Effective People: Powerful Lessons in Personal Change* (New York: Free Press, 1989), 239.

13. Deirdre Sullivan, "Always Go to the Funeral," in *This I Believe: The Personal Philosophies of Remarkable Men and Women,* ed. Jay Allison and Dan Gediman (New York: Holt Paperbacks, 2007), 235–237.

14. Tal Ben-Shahar, Certificate in Positive Psychology Program (online and in-person, Wholebeing Institute, Lenox, MA, February 2014–January 2015).

15. Kyle Benson, "The Magic Relationship Ratio, According to Science," The Gottman Institute, October 4, 2017, https://www.gottman.com/blog/the-magic-relationship-ratio-according-science/.

16. Lindsay Holmes, "The Happiest and Unhappiest Cities in America May Surprise You," *HuffPost,* July 21, 2014, updated December 6, 2017, https://www.huffpost.com/entry/us-unhappiest-cities_n_5606503.

Chapter Five: Mindfulness and Compassion—The Foundations of Happiness

1. Brigid Schulte, "Harvard Neuroscientist: Meditation Not Only Reduces Stress, Here's How It Changes Your Brain," *Washington Post*, May 26, 2015, https://www.washingtonpost.com/news/inspired-life/wp/2015/05/26/harvard-neuroscientist-meditation-not-only-reduces-stress-it-literally-changes-your-brain/.

2. Rick Hanson, PhD, *Hardwiring Happiness: The New Brain Science of Contentment, Calm, and Confidence* (New York: Harmony Books, 2013).

3. "Sunday Morning Worship: No Time For Casual Faith, General Assembly 2018," Unitarian Universalist Association, https://www.uua.org/ga/past/2018/worship/sunday.

4. Sonja Lyubomirsky, *The How of Happiness: A New Approach to Getting the Life You Want* (New York: The Penguin Press, 2007), 241.

5. Anna Almendrala, "The U.S. Surgeon General Wants to Bring You Health Via Happiness," *HuffPost,* November 23, 2015, updated December 20, 2016, https://www.huffpost.com/entry/surgeon-general-happiness-vivek-murthy_n_564f857ee4b0d4093a57c8b0.

6. Piero Ferrucci, *The Power of Kindness: The Unexpected Benefits of Leading a Compassionate Life* (New York: Penguin Group, 2006), 80.

7. Tal Ben-Shahar, Certificate in Positive Psychology Program (online and in-person, Wholebeing Institute, Lenox, MA, February 2014– January 2015).

8. Ellen Langer, interview by Krista Tippett, "Science of Mindlessness and Mindfulness," *On Being,* November 2, 2017, https://onbeing.org/programs/ellen-langer-science-of-mindlessness-and-mindfulness-nov2017/#transcript.

9. Matthieu Ricard, *Happiness: A Guide to Developing Life's Most Important Skill* (New York: Little, Brown and Company, 2003), 45.

10. Jon Kabat-Zinn, *Wherever You Go, There You Are: Mindfulness Meditation in Everyday Life* (New York: Hachette Books, 1994), 4.

11. Jack Kornfield, interview by Rick Hanson, PhD, *The Foundations of Well-Being: Growing the Good in Your Brain and Your Life*, YouTube, May 26, 2015, https://youtu.be/e49wwwmLj74.

12. Trudi Frazel, "What Sustains Your Breath?" *UU World*, August 20, 2018, https://www.uuworld.org/articles/scuba-metaphor.

13. Kabat-Zinn, *Wherever You Go, There You Are*, 5.

14. Helen Keller, "Three Days to See," *The Atlantic Monthly*, vol. 151, no. 1 (January 1933): 35–42.

Chapter Six: You Don't Have to Be the Mermaid—Social Comparison & Empathy

1. Hyman Schactel qtd. in *Wisdom for the Soul: Five Millennia of Prescriptions for Spiritual Healing* by Larry Chang (Washington, DC: Gnosophia Publishers, 2006), 354.

2. "Social Comparison Theory," *Psychology Today*, 2020, https://www.psychologytoday.com/us/basics/social-comparison-theory.

3. Sonja Lyubomirsky, *The How of Happiness: A New Approach to Getting The Life You Want* (New York: Penguin Books, 2007), 116.

4. Loretta G. Breuning, PhD, "Can We Stop Comparing Ourselves to Others?" *Psychology Today*, December 10, 2014, https://www.psychologytoday.com/us/blog/your-neurochemical-self/201412/can-we-stop-comparing-ourselves-others.

5. Lyubomirsky, *The How of Happiness*, 117.

6. Tim Herrera, "Smarter Living," *New York Times,* June 25, 2018, https://static.nytimes.com/email-content/SL_3307.html?nlid=68967808.

7. J. Ian Norris and Jeff Larsen, "Wanting More Than You Have and Its Consequences for Well-Being," Research.Gate, October 2010, https://www.researchgate.net/publication/226039369_Wanting_more_than_you_have_and_it's_Consequences_for_Well-being.

8. Shankar Vedantam, "Feeding the Green-Eyed Monster: What Happens When Envy Turns Ugly," *Hidden Brain,* NPR, February 26, 2018, https://www.npr.org/transcripts/586674547.

9. Tim Herrera, "Smarter Living," *New York Times,* June 25, 2018, https://static.nytimes.com/email-content/SL_3307.html?nlid=68967808.

10. "Meryl Streep > Quotes > Quotable Quote," Goodreads, 2020, https://www.goodreads.com/quotes/83963-the-great-gift-of-human-beings-is-that-we-have.

11. "Maya Angelou Quotes," BrainyQuote, 2020, https://www. brainyquote.com/quotes/maya_angelou_578832.

12. Jeremy Rifkin, "The Empathic Civilisation," RSAnimate | YouTube, May 6, 2010, https://youtu.be/l7AWnfFRc7g.

13. "Empathy: College Students Don't Have As Much As They Used To," *Michigan News*, Office of the Vice President for Communications, University of Michigan, May 27, 2010, https://news.umich.edu/ empathy-college-students-don-t-have-as-much-as-they-used-to/.

14. Tal Ben-Shahar, Certificate in Positive Psychology Program (online and in-person, Wholebeing Institute, Lenox, MA, February 2014–January 2015).

Chapter Seven: The Road to Happiness Includes Frequent Stops in Conflict Land

1. Dalai Lama (@DalaiLama), "One very important factor for sustaining hope," Facebook post, April 13, 2018, https://www.facebook. com/DalaiLama/posts/one-very-important-factor-for-sustaining-hope-is-to-have-an-optimistic-attitude-/10155517272527616./.

2. "Martin Luther King Jr. > Quotes > Quotable Quote," Goodreads, 2020, https://www.goodreads.com/quotes/270483-man-must-evolve-for-all-human-conflict-a-method-which.

3. Ken Cloke, "There Is No Them. There Is Just Us," interview by Awakin Call Editors, *DailyGood: News That Inspires,* November 27, 2017, http://www.dailygood.org/story/1883/ken-cloke-there-is-no-them-there-is-just-us-/.

4. Jonathan Haidt, *The Happiness Hypothesis: Finding Modern Truth in Ancient Wisdom* (New York: Basic Books, 2006), 59–63.

5. Kendra Cherry, "How the Self-Serving Bias Protects Self-Esteem," *Verywell Mind*, August 19, 2019, https://www.verywellmind.com/ what-is-the-self-serving-bias.

Chapter Eight: Forgiveness Is Beautiful

1. Jenna Amatuili, "Forgiveness Ceremony Unites Veterans and Natives at Standing Rock Casino," *HuffPost,* December 6, 2016, https:// www.huffpost.com/entry/forgiveness-ceremony-unites-veterans-and-natives-at-standing-rock-casino_n_5845cdbbe4b055b31398b199.

2.   Piero Ferrucci, *The Power of Kindness: The Unexpected Benefits of Leading a Compassionate Life* (New York: Penguin Group, 2006), 34.

3.   Sonya Lyubomirksy, *The How of Happiness: A New Approach to Getting the Life You Want* (New York: Penguin Books, 2007), 173.

4.   "The Nobel Peace Prize 1993," NobelPrize.org, Nobel Media AB 2020, Sat. 11 Apr 2020. https://www.nobelprize.org/prizes/peace/1993/press-release/.

5.   Joseph Shapiro, "Amish Forgive School Shooter, Struggle with Grief," NPR, October 2, 2007, https://www.npr.org/templates/story/story.php?storyId=14900930.

6.   Ferrucci, *The Power of Kindness*, 32.

7.   Lyubomirsky, *The How of Happiness*, 170.

8.   Lyubomirsky, *The How of Happiness*, 170.

9.   "Forgiveness Defined," *Greater Good Magazine: Science-Based Insights for a Meaningful Life,* The Greater Good Science Center at the University of California Berkeley, 2020, https://greatergood.berkeley.edu/topic/forgiveness/definition.

10. Shapiro, "Amish Forgive School Shooter."

11. Helen Colwell Adams, "Forgiveness Is Not for the Weak," *LancasterOnline*, LNP Media Group, September 20, 2009, https://lancasteronline.com/news/forgiveness-is-not-for-the-weak/article_96014ebc-2a62-5727-a1f2-26d4563787e6.html.

12. "Oprah Winfrey > Quotes > Quotable Quote," *Goodreads,* 2020, https://www.goodreads.com/quotes/376558-forgiveness-is-giving-up-the-hope-that-the-past-could.

13. Fred Luskin, "What Is Forgiveness?" *Greater Good Magazine: Science-Based Insights for a Meaningful Life,* The Greater Good Science Center at the University of California Berkeley, August 19, 2010, https://greatergood.berkeley.edu/article/item/what_is_forgiveness.

14. Fred Luskin, "The Choice to Forgive," The Science of a Meaningful Life Video Series, *Greater Good Magazine: Science-Based Insights for a Meaningful Life,"* The Greater Good Science Center at the University of California Berkeley, September 2010, https://greatergood.berkeley.edu/video/item/the_choice_to_forgive.

15. Lyubomirsky, *The How of Happiness*, 172.

16. Maria Popova, "David Whyte on the True Meaning of Friendship, Love, and Heartbreak," *Brain Pickings*, accessed December 2, 2019, https://www.brainpickings.org/2015/04/29david-whyte-consolations-words/.

17. "Forgiveness Defined," *Greater Good Magazine*.

18. Fred Luskin, "Nine Steps to Forgiveness," *Greater Good Magazine: Science-Based Insights for a Meaningful Life,"* The Greater Good Science Center at the University of California Berkeley, September 1, 2004, https://greatergood.berkeley.edu/article/item/nine_steps_to_forgiveness.

19. Jill Suttie, "Learning Forgiveness in an Unforgiving World," *Greater Good Magazine: Science-Based Insights for a Meaningful Life,"* The Greater Good Science Center at the University of California Berkeley, September 2, 2015, https://greatergood.berkeley.edu/article/item/learning_forgiveness_in_an_unforgiving_world.

20. Dr. Judy Kuriansky, "Martin Luther King Jr. Words of Wisdom: Apply to Your Life," *HuffPost*, January 20, 2014, updated March 22, 2014, https://www.huffpost.com/entry/martin-luther-king-jr-wor_b_4624747.

21. Ferrucci, *The Power of Kindness*, 40.

Chapter Nine: The Interconnected Happiness of Humans and Other Animals

1. Nathan Rott, "What The Trump Administration Has Proposed To Change In The Endangered Species Act," NPR, July 26, 2018, https://www.npr.org/2018/07/26/632771911/what-the-trump-administration-has-proposed-to-change-in-the-endangered-species-a.

2. Jenny Higgins. "Cod Moratorium," Newfoundland & Labrador Heritage, 2009, https://www.heritage.nf.ca/articles/economy/moratorium.php.

3. "Collapse of the Atlantic Northwest Cod Industry," *Wikipedia: The Free Encyclopedia*, Wikimedia Foundation, last modified January 25, 2020, https://en.wikipedia.org/wiki/Collapse_of_the_Atlantic_northwest_cod_fishery.

4. Pam Wright, "Worst Red Tide in More Than a Decade Leaves Droves of Animals Dead on Southwest Florida Beaches," *The Weather*

Channel, July 28, 2018, https://weather.com/science/environment/news/2018-07-28-florida-fort-myers-red-tide-dead-animals-turtles.

5. Angela Fritz, "How Climate Change is Making 'Red Tide' Algal Blooms Even Worse," *The Washington Post*, August 15, 2018, https://www.washingtonpost.com/news/capital-weather-gang/wp/2018/08/14/how-climate-change-is-making-red-tide-algal-blooms-even-worse/.

6. Fritz, "How Climate Change is Making 'Red Tide' Algal Blooms Even Worse."

7. Kent McFarland, "Outdoor Radio: Tracking Moose Health," Vermont Center for Ecostudies, March 26, 2018, https://vtecostudies.org/blog/outdoor-radio-tracking-moose-health/.

8. Ron Krupp, "Forest Fragmentation Threatens Bird Diversity," VPR, June 26, 2018, https://www.vpr.org/post/forest-fragmentation-threatens-bird-diversity#stream/0.

9. Jonathan Safran Foer, *Eating Animals* (New York Little, Brown and Company, 2009), 139.

10. Beth Allgood, Marina Ratchford and Kate Lang, *Measuring What Matters: True Wellbeing for Animals and People*, International Fund for Animal Welfare (IFAW), December 2016.

11. Ginny Sassaman, "True Well-Being for Animals and People: Presentation by GNHUSA Board Member Beth Allgood," GNHUSA, September 4, 2017, https://gnhusa.org/gnhusa-news/true-well-animals-people-presentation-gnhusa-board-member-beth-allgood/.

12. Elizabeth Pennisi, "Three Billion North American Birds Have Vanished Since 1970, Surveys Show," *Science*, American Association for the Advancement of Science, September 19, 2019, https://www.sciencemag.org/news/2019/09/three-billion-north-american-birds-have-vanished-1970-surveys-show.

13. National Oceanic and Atmospheric Administration, "North Atlantic Right Whale," NOAA Fisheries, accessed December 5, 2019, https://www.fisheries.noaa.gov/species/north-atlantic-right-whale.

14. Sassaman, "True Well-Being for Animals and People."

15. Nicholas Kristof, "Choosing Animals Over People?" *New York Times Opinion*, April 7, 2018, https://www.nytimes.com/2018/04/07/opinion/sunday/wildlife-central-african-republic.html.

16. Allgood, Ratchford and Lange, *Measuring What Matters.*

17. Sherri Mitchell, *Sacred Instructions: Indigenous Wisdom for Living Spirit-Based Change* (Berkeley: North Atlantic Books, 2018), 9.

Chapter Ten: Kindness—Our Best Tool for Personal and Collective Wholeness

1. Piero Ferrucci, *The Power of Kindness: The Unexpected Benefits of Leading a Compassionate Life* (New York: Jeremy P. Tharcher/ Penguin, 2006), 2.

2. Caroline Bologna, "'Kindness Is Everything' Signs Promote Love In Response To Hate," *HuffPost,* March 8, 2017, updated March 24, 2017, https://www.huffpost.com/entry/kindness-is-everything-signs-promote-love-in-response-to-hate_n_587f9149e4b0c147f0bc1cf1.

3. "Forget Survival of the Fittest: It Is Kindness That Counts," *Scientific American,* February 26, 2009, https://www.scientificamerican.com/article/kindness-emotions-psychology/.

4. Temple Grandin and Catherine Johnson, *Animals in Translation: Using the Mysteries of Autism to Decode Animal Behavior* (New York: Scribner Books, 2005), 24.

5. Kim Childs, "Giving Thanks 365 Days a Year," Wholebeing Institute, 2019, https://wholebeinginstitute.com/giving-thanks-365-days-year/.

6. Katy Brennan, "Kindness Isn't Just Courtesy—for Buddhists, it's a Moral Discipline," Global Light Minds, May 4, 2013, http://www.globallightminds.com/2013/05/weekend-meditation-on-kindness/.

7. Ferrucci, *The Power of Kindness*, 8.

8. Alex Dixon, "Kindness Makes You Happy … and Happiness Makes You Kind," *Greater Good Magazine: Science-Based Insights for a Meaningful Life,* The Greater Good Science Center at the University of California Berkeley, September 6, 2011, https://greatergood.berkeley.edu/article/itemkindness_makes_you_happy_and_happiness_makes_you_kind.

9. Sonja Lyubomirsky, *The How of Happiness: A New Approach to Getting the Life You Want* (New York: Penguin Books, 2007), 129–130.

10. Birju Pandya, "5 Ways Science Says Kindness Will Change Your Life," Awaken, September 2, 2019, https://www.awaken.com/2019/09/5-ways-science-says-kindness-will-change-your-life/.

11. John O'Donohue, "Kindness: The First Gift," *DailyGood: News That Inspires,* November 28, 2014, http://www.dailygood.org/story/899/kindness-the-first-gift.

12. Adam Phillips and Barbara Taylor, *On Kindness* (New York: Picador, 2009), 6.

13. Karyn Hall, PhD, "The Importance of Kindness," *Psychology Today,* December 4, 2017, https://www.psychologytoday.com/us/blog/pieces-mind/201712/the-importance-kindness.

14. Phillips and Taylor, *On Kindness,* 9.

15. Maria Popova, "How Kindness Became Our Forbidden Pleasure," Brain Pickings, accessed December 12, 2019, https://www.brainpickings.org/2015/07/13/on-kindness-adam-phillips-barbara-taylor/.

16. Annie Lowrey, "America's Epidemic of Unkindness," *The Atlantic,* November 28, 2019, https://www.theatlantic.com/ideas/archive/2019/11/how-be-kind/602488.

17. Ta-Nehisi Coates, *Between the World and Me* (New York: Spiegel & Grau, 2015), 126.

18. Rick Hanson, PhD, "What Can I Do: Do Not Underestimate the Impact of a Small Deed," *Psychology Today,* September 6, 2016, https://www.psychologytoday.com/za/blog/your-wise-brain/201609/what-can-i-do.

19. Dalai Lama Quotes, "Be Kind," BrainyQuote, BrainyMedia, Inc., 2001–2020, https://www.brainyquote.com/quotes/dalai_lama_378036.

Chapter Eleven: Attitude of Gratitude

1. Eric Barker, "Happy Thoughts: Here Are the Things Proven To Make You Happier," *Time Guide to Happiness,* Time USA, LLC, 2020, https://time.com/collection/guide-to-happiness/49947/happy-thoughts-here-are-the-things-proven-to-make-you-happier/.

2. Anna Almendrala, "The Surgeon General on Health Via Happiness," *DailyGood: News That Inspires,* December 8, 2015, http://www.dailygood.org/story/1176/the-surgeon-general-on-health-via-happiness/.

Endnotes

3. Robert A. Emmons, PhD, *The Little Book of Gratitude: Create a Life of Happiness and Wellbeing by Giving Thanks* (London: Gaia Books, 2016), 7.

4. Gregor Claus, Wouter Vanhove, Patrick Van Damme and Guy Smagghe, "Challenges in Cocoa Pollination: The Case of Côte d'Ivoire," Intech Open, Limited, March 15, 2018, https://https://cdn.intechopen.com/pdfs/59982.pdf.

5. Robert Emmons, "Why Gratitude Is Good," *Greater Good Magazine: Science-Based Insights for a Meaningful Life,* The Greater Good Science Center at the University of California Berkeley, November 16, 2010, https://greatergood.berkeley.edu/article/item/why_gratitude_is_good.

6. Ed Diener and Robert Biswas-Diener, *Happiness: Unlocking the Mysteries of Psychological Wealth* (Malden: Blackwell Publishing, 2008), 151-152.

7. "David Steindl-Rast > Quotes," Goodreads, 2020, https://www.goodreads.com/author/quotes/4182.David_Steindl_Rast.

8. Piero Ferrucci, *The Power of Kindness: The Unexpected Benefits of Leading a Compassionate Life* (New York: Jeremy P. Tharcher/Penguin, 2006), 176.

9. Claire Bates, "Is This the World's Happiest Man? Brain Scans Reveal French Monk Has 'Abnormally Large Capacity' for Joy - Thanks to Meditation," *Daily Mail.com,* Associated Newspapers, Ltd., October 31, 2012, https://www.dailymail.co.uk/health/article-2225634/Is-worlds-happiest-man-Brain-scans-reveal-French-monk-abnormally-large-capacity-joy-meditation.html.

10. Emmons, *The Little Book of Gratitude.*

11. Rick Hanson, PhD, *Positive Neuroplasticity Training*, Online Course Notes, September 2017.

12. Tal Ben-Shahar, "Big Think Interview with Tal Ben-Shahar," Big Think, October 2, 2009, https://bigthink.com/videos/big-think-interview-with-tal-ben-shahar.

13. Emmons, "Why Gratitude Is Good."

14. David Steindl-Rast, "Anatomy of Gratitude," interview by Krista Tippett, *On Being,* January 21, 2016, updated December 21, 2017, https://onbeing.org/programs/david-steindl-rast-anatomy-of-gratitude-dec2017/.

15. Oliver Sacks, *Gratitude* (New York: Alfred A. Knopf, 2015), 16.

16. Christina N. Armenta and Sonja Lyubomirsky, "How Gratitude Motivates Us to Become Better People," *Greater Good Magazine: Science-Based Insights for a Meaningful Life,* The Greater Good Science Center at the University of California Berkeley, May 23, 2017, https://greatergood.berkeley.edu/article/item/how_gratitude_motivates_us_to_become_better_people.

17. Kerry Howells, "How Can Our Gratitude Contribute to World Peace?" *DailyGood: News That Inspires,* January 9, 2018, http://www.dailygood.org/story/1868/how-can-our-gratitude-contribute-to-world-peace-kerry-howells/.

Chapter Twelve: Reading, Writing, Social Justice—and Happiness

1. "Five Ways to Wellbeing: The Evidence," New Economics Foundation, October 22, 2008, https://neweconomics.org/2008/10/five-ways-to-wellbeing-the-evidence.

2. "Five Ways to Wellbeing: The Postcards," New Economics Foundation, October 21, 2008, https://neweconomics.org/2008/10/five-ways-to-wellbeing-the-postcards.

3. Sonja Lyubomirsky, *The How of Happiness: A New Approach to Getting the Life You Want* (New York: The Penguin Press, 2007), 184–185.

4. "About Us," Action for Happiness, accessed January 10, 2020, https://www.actionforhappiness.org/about-us.

5. "10 Keys to Happier Living: Keep Learning New Things," Action for Happiness, accessed January 10, 2020, https://www.actionforhappiness.org/10-keys-to-happier-livingkeep-learning-new-things/details.

6. Margaret J. Wheatley, *Who Do We Choose to Be? Facing Reality, Claiming Leadership, Restoring Sanity* (Oakland: Berrett-Koehler, 2017), 124–125.

7. Nic Marks, "The Happy Planet Index," TED: Ideas Worth Spreading, July 2010, https://www.ted.com/talks/nic_marks_the_happy_planet_index.

8. Maria Popova, "Rebecca Solnit's Lovely Letter to Children About How Books Solace, Empower, and Transform Us," Brain Pickings, accessed February 9, 2020, https://www.brainpickings. org/2019/01/03/a-velocity-of-being-rebecca-solnit/.

9. "Poems About Life Lessons: Poems About Lessons Learned from Mistakes," FamilyFriend Poems, 2006–2020, https://www.family friendpoems.com/poems/life/lesson/.

10. Marcus Rediker, "The 'Quaker Comet' Was the Greatest Abolitionist You've Never Heard Of," *Smithsonian Magazine*, September 2017, https://www.smithsonianmag.com/history/quaker-comet-greatest-abolitionist-never-heard-180964401/.

11. Jill Lepore, *These Truths: A History of the United States* (New York: W.W. Norton and Company, 2018), 72–76.

12. Lepore, *These Truths*, 74.

Chapter Thirteen: When Mother Nature Ain't Happy

1. "Great Lakes Plastic Pollution: Fighting for Plastic-free Water," Alliance for the Great Lakes, 2020, https://greatlakes.org/great-lakes-plastic-pollution-fighting-for-plastic-free-water/.

2. Lucy Purdy, "£10m Fund to Plant More Than 130,000 Trees in England's Urban Areas," *Positive News*, May 20, 2019, https://www. positive.news/environment/10m-fund-to-plant-more-than-130000-trees-in-englands-urban-areas/.

3. "The View From Above: Why Our Future May Depend on the Fate of Birds," Paid for and Posted by Allbirds, *New York Times*, 2020, https://www.nytimes.com/paidpost/allbirds/the-view-from-above.html.

4. John McPhee, *The Control of Nature* (New York: Farrar, Straus and Giroux), 1989.

5. John Crowe Ransom, "Introduction: A Statement of Principles; Reconstructed but Unregenerate," *I'll Take My Stand: The South and the Agrarian Tradition* (New York: Harper, 1930), 9.

6. Margaret Renkl, "Effortless Environmentalism: Here Are Some Easy Ways to Live More Gently on the Earth. The Key Word Here Is 'Easy'" the *New York Times Opinion,* January 13, 2020, https:// www.nytimes.com/2020/01/13/opinion/earth-environmentalism.html.

7. "Welcome to Happiness: Here to Empower You in Happiness," Happiness Alliance, accessed February 9, 2020, https://www.happy counts.org/.

8. Happiness Alliance, "Earth Day Happiness: Happiness Data Report for Earth Day 2019," Thrive Global, April 22, 2019, https://thrive global.com/stories/earth-day-happiness/.

9. Dr. Qing Li, "'Forest Bathing' Is Great for Your Health. Here's How to Do It," *Time*, Time USA, LLC, May 1, 2018, https://time. com/5259602/japanese-forest-bathing/.

10. "Science Agrees: Nature Is Good for You," Association of Nature & Forest Therapy Guides & Programs, 2019, https://www.natureand foresttherapy.org/about/science.

11. Jill Suttie, "Why Is Nature So Good for Your Mental Health?" *Greater Good Magazine: Science-Based Insights for a Meaningful Life,* The Greater Good Science Center at the University of California Berkeley, April 19, 2019, https://greatergood.berkeley.edu/article/ item/why_is_nature_so_good_for_your_mental_health.

12. Christiane Northrup, MD, "The Farm Effect: How Dirt Makes You Happy and Healthy," Christiane Northrup, Inc., March 1, 2016, https://www.drnorthrup.com/dirt-strenthens-immune-system-happier-healthier/.

13. Jamie Feldmar, "Gardening Could Be the Hobby That Helps You Live to 100," BBC: Generation Project, December 10, 2018, https:// www.bbc.com/worklife/article/20181210-gardening-could-be-the-hobby-that-helps-you-live-to-100.

14. Oliver Sacks, "The Healing Power of Gardens," *New York Times Opinion,* April 18, 2019, https://www.nytimes.com/2019/04/18/opin-ion/sunday/oliver-sacks-gardens.html.

15. Andrew Weil, MD, "Is Nature Deficit Disorder Real?" WEIL, October 7, 2011, https://www.drweil.com/health-wellness/ balanced-living/healthy-living/is-nature-deficit-disorder-real/.

16. Christopher Bergland, "Childhood Exposure to Nature May Have Long-Lasting Benefits," *Psychology Today,* May 26, 2019, https:// www.psychologytoday.com/us/blog/the-athletes-way/201905/ childhood-exposure-nature-may-have-long-lasting-benefits.

17. Jill Suttie, "How to Protect Kids from Nature-Deficit Disorder," *Greater Good Magazine: Science-Based Insights for a Meaningful*

Life, The Greater Good Science Center at the University of California Berkeley, September 15, 2016, https://greatergood.berkeley.edu/article/item/how_to_protect_kids_from_nature_deficit_disorder.

Chapter Fourteen: The Extraordinary Value of Everyday Beauty

1. Piero Ferrucci, *Beauty and the Soul: The Extraordinary Power of Everyday Beauty to Heal Your Life* (New York: Penguin Group, 2009), xiv–xv.

2. From the Navajo Indians of North America, Reading #682, *Singing the Living Tradition* (Boston: Unitarian Universalist Association, 1993).

3. Minot Judson Savage, "Seek Not Afar for Beauty," *Singing the Living Tradition* (Boston: Unitarian Universalist Association, 1993), 77.

4. Robert F. Kennedy, "Remarks at the University of Kansas, March 18, 1968," John F. Kennedy Presidential Library and Museum, accessed January 18, 2020, https://www.jfklibrary.org/learn/about-jfk/the-kennedy-family/robert-f-kennedy/robert-f-kennedy-speeches/remarks-at-the-university-of-kansas-march-18-1968.

5. "The 24 Character Strengths," VIA Institute on Character, 2020, https://www.viacharacter.org/character-strengths.

6. Cody C. Delistraty, "The Beauty-Happiness Connection: Looking at Lovely Things—and People—Can Improve Quality of Life," *The Atlantic,* August 15, 2014, https://www.theatlantic.com/health/archive/2014/08/the-beautyhappiness-connection/375678/.

7. Mihir Zaveri, "Black Women Now Hold Crowns in 5 Major Beauty Pageants," *New York Times,* December 15, 2019, https://www.nytimes.com/2019/12/15/style/black-women-win-beauty-pageants.html.

8. Jonathan Kozol, "Schools Without Beauty," *Greater Good Magazine: Science-Based Insights for a Meaningful Life*, The Greater Good Science Center at the University of California Berkeley, September 1, 2005, https://greatergood.berkeley.edu/article/item/schools_without_beauty.

9. John O'Donohue, "The Inner Landscape of Beauty," interview by Krista Tippett, *On Being*, August 31, 2017, https://onbeing.org/programs/john-odonohue-the-inner-landscape-of-beauty-aug2017/.

10. Jen Wolfe, "The Concept of Hózhó," October 19, 2014, in Marti Beddoe, "What is Hózhó? What is the Beauty Way?" Designs For Peace: Practices for Sustaining Lives of Meaning, Joy, and Beauty, October 23, 2017, https://martibeddoe.com/blog/2017/10/23/what-is-hozho-what-is-the-beauty-way/.

11. Ferrucci, *Beauty and the Soul.*

12. "With Liberty, Justice … and Beauty for All," And Beauty for All, accessed January 19, 2020, https://www.andbeautyforall.org/.

13. John de Graaf, NAPA Watersheds speech email message to author, July 7, 2019.

14. Rick Hanson, PhD, "Find Beauty—Just One Thing," YouTube, April 24, 2012, https://youtu.be/AmmPHPeCVpQ.

Chapter Fifteen: Creativity—Save the Planet, Produce a Masterpiece, or Just Have Fun

1. "Champlain Beach Rocks," Shelburne Farms: Learning for a Sustainable Future, accessed January 22, 2020, https://shelburnefarms.org/blog/champlain-beach-rocks.

2. Demian Farnworth, "What Is Creativity? 21 Authentic Definitions You'll Love," Copyblogger, Copyblogger Media, LLC, April 11, 2016, https://copyblogger.com/define-creativity/.

3. "What is Creativity? (And Why Is It a Crucial Factor for Business Success?)," Creativity at Work, 1999–2020, https://www.creativityatwork.com/2014/02/17/what-is-creativity/.

4. Maria Popova, *Brain Pickings*, quoted in Farnworth, "What is Creativity? 21 Authentic."

5. Peter Koestenbaum, quoted in Julia Cameron with Mark Bryan, *The Artist's Way: A Spiritual Path to Higher Creativity* (New York: Jeremy P. Tarcher/Putnam, 1992), 3.

6. Sonia Simone, quoted in Farnworth, "What is Creativity? 21 Authentic."

7. Brenda Ueland, quoted in Cameron with Bryan, *The Artist's Way*, 4.

8. Elizabeth Gilbert, *Big Magic: Creative Living Beyond Fear* (New York: Riverhead Books, 2015), 89.

9. "Dieter F. Uchtdorf > Quotes > Quotable Quote," Goodreads, 2020, https://www.goodreads.com/quotes/8070701-the-desire-to-create-is-one-of-the-deepest-yearnings.

10. John Geirland, "Go with the Flow," *Wired*, September 1, 1996, https://www.wired.com/1996/09/czik/.

11. Twyla Tharp, *The Creative Habit: Learn It and Use It for Life* (New York: Simon and Schuster, 2003).

12. Farnworth, "What is Creativity? 21 Authentic."

13. Mihaly Csikszentmihalyi, "Flow, the Secret to Happiness," TED: Ideas Worth Spreading, February 2004, https://www.ted.com/talks/mihaly_csikszentmihalyi_flow_the_secret_to_happiness.

14. Dr. Robert Epstein, *Creativity Games for Trainers: A Handbook of Group Activities for Jumpstarting Workplace Creativity* (New York: McGraw-Hill, 1996), 25–28.

15. "Dr. Robert Epstein—Understanding the Creative Process," *CNBC*, June 23, 2008, updated August 5, 2010, https://www.cnbc.com/id/25338958.

16. Roger von Oech, *A Whack on the Side of the Head: How You Can Be More Creative* (Menlo Park: Creative Think, 1983), 167–174.

17. "Fear is Boring and Other Tips for Living a Creative Life: Elizabeth Gilbert Shares 11 Ways to Think Smartly About Creativity," IDEAS.TED.COM, Ted Conferences, LLC, September 24, 2015, https://ideas.ted.com/fear-is-boring-and-other-tips-for-living-a-creative-life/.

18. Jill Suttie, "Doing Something Creative Can Boost your Well-Being," *Greater Good Magazine: Science-Based Insights for a Meaningful Life,* The Greater Good Science Center at the University of California Berkeley, March 21, 2017, https://greatergood.berkeley.edu/article/item/doing_something_creative_can_boost_your_well_being.

19. Peggy Taylor and Charlie Murphy, syndicated from *Yes Magazine,* "Ten Things Creative People Know," *DailyGood: News That Inspires,* June 5, 2014, http://www.dailygood.org/story/766/ten-things-creative-people-know-peggy-taylor-charlie-murphy/.

20. "Volkswagen: Fun Theory Piano Staircase," *AdAge: The Creativity Newsletter,* October 5, 2009, https://adage.com/creativity/work/fun-theory-piano-staircase/17522.

21. The Hitching Post Vermont Facebook Group, "The Hitching Post: Creating Imaginative Alternatives to Single-occupied Vehicles," The Hitching Post, accessed January 27, 2020, https://www.thehitching post.org.

22. Gustavo Henrique Ruffo, "Remember the Solar Road in France? It Was a Disaster," InsideEVs, August 14, 2019, https://insideevs.com/news/365186/solar-road-france-fiasco/.

23. Daniel T. Cross, "A Sun-powered Bicycle Path Glows in the Dark in Poland," *Sustainability Times,* April 15, 2019, https://www.sustain ability-times.com/clean-cities/a-sun-powered-bicycle-path-glows-in-the-dark-in-poland/.

24. Susannah Clifford Blachly, "Colored Balloons," YouTube, December 12, 2012, https://youtu.be/Zfqq4qs703U.

Chapter Sixteen: Calling All Happiness Prophets—Accessing Our Sacred Instructions to Create a Better World

1. Joan Chittister, *The Time Is Now: A Call to Uncommon Courage* (New York: Convergent Books, 2019), 15.

2. Sherri Mitchell, *Sacred Instructions: Indigenous Wisdom for Living Spirit-Based Change* (Berkeley: North Atlantic Books, 2018), xix–xx.

3. "Stefano Bartolini," The Happiness Roundtable, accessed January 29, 2020, https://www.happinessroundtable.org/stefano-bartolini.html.

4. "History," Local Futures: Economics of Happiness, International Society for Ecology and Culture, 2020, https://www.localfutures.org/about/history/.

5. Helena Norberg-Hodge, *Local Is Our Future: Steps to an Economics of Happiness* (Local Futures, 2019), 9.

6. Kathleen Foody, "Jimmy Carter: World at 'Turning Point,' Must Commit to Peace," *The Seattle Times,* June 20, 2016, https://www.seattletimes.com/nation-world/jimmy-carter-world-at-turning-point-must-commit-to-peace/.

7. Margaret J. Wheatley, *Who Do We Choose to Be? Facing Reality, Claiming Leadership, Restoring Sanity* (Oakland: Berrett-Koehler, 2017), 36.

8. Wheatley, *Who Do We Choose to Be?*, 7.

9. Edward J. Watts, interview by David Folkenflik, "What Americans Can Learn From the Fall of the Roman Republic," *On Point*, January 11, 2019, https://www.wbur.org/onpoint/2019/01/11/america-rome-republic-lessons.

10. Neil Steinberg, "Crumbling US Senate Echoes Roman Collapse," *Chicago Sun-Times*, February 2, 2020, https://chicago.suntimes.com/columnists/2020/2/2/21119032/crumbling-us-senate-echoes-roman-collapse-trump.

11. Paul Gilding, *The Great Disruption: Why the Climate Crisis Will Bring On the End of Shopping and the Birth of a New World* (New York: Bloomsbury Press, 2011).

12. Gilding, *The Great Disruption*, 8.

13. Arundhati Roy, *Ordinary Person's Guide To Empire* (Boston: South End Press, 2004), 86.

14. "Albert Einstein > Quotes > Quotable Quote," Goodreads, 2020, https://www.goodreads.com/quotes/6702623-a-new-type-of-thinking-is-essential-if-mankind-is.

15. Martin Luther King, Jr., *Strength to Love* (New York: Harper & Row, 1963).

16. Maria Sirois, PsyD, "So Much Rests," Maria Sirois Mailing List, email message to author, June 27, 2019.

17. "Character Strengths," VIA Institute on Character, 2020, https://www.viacharacter.org/character-strengths-via.

18. "The 24 Character Strengths," VIA Institute, 2020, https://www.viacharacter.org/character-strengths.

19. Jill Suttie, "Why We Should Seek Happiness Even in Hard Times: Jack Kornfield Shares His Wisdom," *Greater Good Magazine: Science-Based Insights for a Meaningful Life*, The Greater Good Science Center at the University of California Berkeley, January 4, 2019, https://greatergood.berkeley.edu/article/item/why_we_should_seek_happiness_even_in_hard_times.

20. "About the Next System Project," The Next System Project, The Democracy Collaborative, 2020, https://thenextsystem.org/about-next-system-project.

21. Arthur Dobrin, DSW, "Happiness Is How You Are, Not How You Feel," *Psychology Today,* January 25, 2013, https://www.psychology today.com/us/blog/am-i-right/201301/happiness-is-how-you-are-not-how-you-feel.

22. Paula Francis, "The Divine in the Data," Gross National Happiness USA, June 17, 2019, https://gnhusa.org/the-happiness-walk/the-divine-in-the-data/.

23. Wheatley, *Who Do We Choose To Be?*, 24.

24. J.R.R. Tolkien, *The Fellowship of the Ring* (New York: Ballantine Books, 1965), 82.

25. Efrat Shani and Yaron Golan, *The Coaching Game* (Udim, Israel: Points of You™, 2007).

About the Author

Elizabeth McNally

GINNY SASSAMAN, MS, CiPP is a co-founder, past president, and advisory board member of Gross National Happiness USA, and the creator of the Happiness Paradigm. Since 2013, she has served as a lay preacher at Unitarian Universalist churches in Vermont, Massachusetts, Wisconsin, and South Carolina. Originally from central Pennsylvania, Ginny and her husband spent many years living in Washington, DC, before settling near Montpelier, Vermont, in 2001. She has a master's in mediation and a certificate in positive psychology, and teaches secular meditation classes. Her website is www. happinessparadigm.com.

Also Available from Rootstock Publishing

The Atomic Bomb on My Back
Taniguchi Sumiteru

Blue Desert
Celia Jeffries

China in Another Time:
A Personal Story
Claire Malcolm Lintilhac

Fly with A Murder of Crows:
A Memoir
Tuvia Feldman

Junkyard at No Town
J.C. Myers

The Language of Liberty:
A Citizen's Vocabulary
Edwin C. Hagenstein

The Lost Grip: Poems
Eva Zimet

Lucy Dancer
Story and Illustrations by Eva Zimet

Nobody Hitchhikes Anymore
Ed Griffin-Nolan

'ed Scare in the Green Mountains:
mont in the McCarthy Era
-1960
Vinston

Safe as Lightning: Poems
Scudder H. Parker

Street of Storytellers
Doug Wilhelm

Tales of Bialystok: A Jewish Journey
from Czarist Russia to America
Charles Zachariah Goldberg

To the Man in the Red Suit: Poems
Christina Fulton

Uncivil Liberties: A Novel
Bernie Lambek

The Violin Family
Melissa Perley; Illustrated by
Fiona Lee Maclean

Wave of the Day: Collected Poems
Mary Elizabeth Winn

Whole Worlds Could Pass Away:
Collected Stories
Rickey Gard Diamond

For more information or
to request a catalog please visit
www.rootstockpublishing.com